THE ROLE OF DISBELIEF IN MARK

· · · · · · · · · · · · · · · · · ·

A New Approach to the Second Gospel

Mary R. Thompson, S.S.M.N.

From the
Library of:

Brother Mark McVann
F.S.C.

Paulist Press New York/Mahwah

The Publisher gratefully acknowledges use of the following materials: Excerpts from Rudolf Bultmann's *The History of the Synoptic Traditions,* revised ed., trans. by John Marsh, copyright © 1968. Used by permission of Basil Blackwell. Excerpts from Donald Juel's *Messiah and Temple,* SBL Dissertation Series 31, copyright © 1977. Used by permission of Scholars Press. Excerpts from Werner H. Kelber's *The Passion in Mark,* copyright © 1976. Used by permission of Fortress Press. Excerpts from William L. Lane's *Commentary on the Gospel of Mark* from *The New International Commentary on the New Testament,* F.F. Bruce, general ed., copyright © 1974. Used by permission of Wm. B. Eerdman's Publishing. Excerpts from Dennis E. Nineham's *Saint Mark,* copyright © 1963. Used by permission of Penguin Books. The Bible text is from the Revised Standard Version Bible, copyright 1946, 1952, 1971 by the Division of Christian Education of the National Council of the Churches of Christ in the USA, and is used by permission.

Book design: Ellen Whitney
Copyright 1989 by Mary R. Thompson, S.S.M.N.

Library of Congress Cataloging-in-Publication Data

Thompson, Mary R., 1928–
    The role of disbelief in Mark : a new approach to the second gospel / by Mary R. Thompson.
      p. cm.
    Bibliography: p.
    Includes index.
    ISBN 0-8091-3044-0 (pbk.) : $7.95 (est.)
    1. Bible. N.T. Mark—Criticism, interpretation, etc. I. Title.
BS2585.2.T475 1989
226'.306—dc 19   88-29114
                                                CIP

Published by Paulist Press
997 Macarthur Boulevard
Mahwah, NJ 07430

Printed and bound in the
United States of America

Table of Contents

Acknowledgments

This work on the gospel of Mark evolved from a New Testament Seminar conducted by Dr. E. P. Sanders at McMaster University, Hamilton, Ontario, in 1984. Much of the work in this study progressed under his careful supervision. I am deeply grateful to Dr. Sanders for his academic guidance and above all for his personal interest in the project and for his encouragement. His incisive comments and patient reading of the text have added much to the finished work.

I am also greatly indebted to Dr. Stephen Westerholm who took time from a very busy schedule to read and to comment. His constructive criticisms and careful editing are very much appreciated.

Dr. Linda Hutcheon of the Department of English at McMaster was also gracious and helpful in reading and making suggestions. Her comments have added much to the literary dimensions of the work. Her patient editing was very helpful.

I owe a special debt of gratitude to my religious community, the Sisters of Saint Mary of Namur, who allowed me the time to do the work and who supported and encouraged me in it.

Mary R. Thompson, S.S.M.N.
Kenmore, New York

Foreword

The gospels of Matthew, Mark and Luke have been subjected to a great deal of close scrutiny during the past two hundred years. Problems which had seemed minimal before that time became the subject of serious study. In 1778 the posthumous publication of Hermann S. Reimarus' "fragment" entitled *Von den Zweck Jesus und seinen Junger,* one of several studies he had written because he had discerned problems with the historical nature of the gospels, signaled the beginning of the quest for the historical Jesus. The concern of the quest writers was to penetrate behind the christology of the gospels and to reach the real historical Jesus. The first phase of the quest came to an end with Albert Schweitzer's *The Quest of the Historical Jesus.*[1] Schweitzer summarized the scholarship up until his own book and concluded that modern day students of the New Testament could not separate the apocalyptic and didactic elements of the gospels from the picture therein presented of the historical Jesus. He wrote:

> Jesus means something to our world because a mighty spiritual force streams forth from him and flows through our time also. The fact can neither be shaken nor confirmed by any historical discovery. It is the solid foundation of Christianity.[2]

Schweitzer's work ended the first phase of the search for the historical Jesus.

The problems raised by the quest scholars did not go away, however, and a second phase ensued. The basic question these scholars sought to answer was, again, the relationship between faith understandings and the picture of Jesus found in the gospels. These seekers of the historical Jesus asked,

"What true historical content can be discerned in these gospels?" Many of the problems concerning the historical Jesus remain unresolved but the process of study which evolved from the attempts to answer them enable the contemporary New Testament scholar to look with some degree of openness and objectivity at the gospels as they now exist and to attempt to discern the objectives of those who formulated them.

One of the important disciplines which has become helpful in discerning the true nature of the gospel picture of Jesus is called redaction criticism. The redaction critic studies the way each evangelist has rewritten and restructured his material in order to present a particular insight into the portrait of Jesus. For example, no one today doubts that, as the redaction critics have proposed, the writer of Mark's gospel intended to stress the sufferings of Jesus. Redaction critics looked at the completed text of the Markan gospel and discerned structures and theological presuppositions which inform those structures. This study of Mark's gospel is based upon the results of redactional critical works which have restored a healthy respect for the completed text.

The gospel of Mark has always played a key role in New Testament studies. For much of the twentieth century scholars have worked on the premise that Mark was the earliest of the gospels and was available to Matthew and Luke as a source for their gospels. Contemporary students of the "synoptic problem" are proposing that there may have been multiple sources for all of our gospels and that knowledge about these is, and is likely to remain, speculative.[3]

At the present time there is a resurgence of interest in the literary character of Mark's narrative. It would be fairly simple to compile an extensive bibliography of material on the literary aspects of Mark's gospel such as its nature as story, the roles of various characters and groups of characters in Mark, and the structural patterns of the gospel. There can be such voluminous writing because the gospel of Mark is a true literary document, and literary documents invite continuing analysis since there are always new meanings to be discovered.

This study of the role of negation, of failure, in Mark's portrayal of Jesus owes its inception to Philip Shuler's research into the literary problem of the nature of the gospels in *A Genre for the Gospels*.[4] Shuler argues that the gospel of Matthew fits the genre of laudatory biography which was common in the ancient world. He suggests that Mark fits the same pattern. The study received added impetus from several authors' comments on the use of irony in Mark.[5] It reflects some of the emphases in the rhetorical critical method currently evolving in biblical research.

Because so much work has already been done on the synoptic gospels as a group and on Mark in particular, it is now possible to propose a holistic reading of the gospel which employs the methods as well as the findings of previous scholarship. This study will pursue a holistic reading of Mark's gospel—horizontally, in the portrait of Jesus in Chapter 3, and, vertically, in Chapters 4, 5 and 6 which present evidence of negative elements in Mark's portrayal of Jesus.

The insight this study intends to explain is that there is so much negation in Mark's gospel, so many negative results, so many failures, that a complete level of negation can be seen to function in it. The proof of this contention requires a holistic reading by its very nature. To be called a "level of meaning" the motif must pervade the entire text. The entire text of Mark's gospel will be perused for evidence of this negative level of meaning which is kept in tension with the affirmative level, as the author obviously intended, in order to produce one portrait of Jesus who is successful on the affirmative level and a failure on the negative level.

There have been many attempts to study the use of negation in Mark, studies of the messianic secret, of the incomprehension of the disciples, of the failure of Jesus with his family. All have been limited to one aspect of the negation and have, therefore, not assessed the total effect of the over-all motif. One reason for the failure to discern the whole motif is the fact that scholars seem to have felt compelled to make it all come out right in the end. In order to do this, they have consistently had to subsume the negative into the affirmative.

A long term result of studying negation as a level of meaning in Mark's gospel could be to open a door to a freer way of reading that gospel. It may free those who study Mark from the task of making it all come out right. For example, they will be able to take the final verse of the gospel literally and to look honestly at its meanings within the text. The present work is based upon the conviction that what the Markan author actually wrote must be taken very seriously and that conclusions predetermined by convictions formed outside the text must be avoided to the extent that that is possible.

Notes

[1] Albert Schweitzer, *The Quest of the Historical Jesus* (London and New York, 1922).

[2] Ibid. p. 397.

[3] See below, Chapter 1.

[4] Philip Shuler, *A Genre for the Gospels* (Philadelphia, 1982).

[5] Wayne Booth, *A Rhetoric of Irony* (Chicago, 1974); Robert Fowler, *Loaves and Fishes* (Missoula, 1981).

Chapter 1

THE NATURE OF MARK'S GOSPEL

· · ·　　　　　　　　　　　　　　　　　　　· · ·

Introduction

The publication of William Wrede's *The Messianic Secret* in 1901[1] opened doors to new methods of studying the synoptic gospels. These methods no longer dealt exclusively with attempts to track down historical facts. Many of these studies, from the time after Wrede, attempted to explain such devices as secrecy commands, the use of doublets and triplets, the incomprehension of the disciples and similar motifs and structures. This study builds upon those developments and examines a whole range of devices in the Markan gospel to ascertain if there is, indeed, an explanation for the use of apparently contradictory elements such as a complete level of affirmation and an equally complete level of negation.

The Background of Markan Criticism

Prior to the modern era biblical literary scholarship had concerned itself primarily with questions such as the authorship and date of a text, sources of the text and like textual[2] matters. Biblical literary criticism has moved, along with the criticism practiced by students of other types of literature, to careful consideration of form and content, their relationship to each other, and analyses of various devices relevant to the meaning.[3] The ultimate purpose of much modern literary criticism and of some modern biblical criticism is to understand the text, qua text, more fully rather than to study sources, history and like matters.

Wrede demonstrated that Mark's gospel was not a simple biography and that a theological concept could have been a controlling factor in the formulation of it.[4] He thereby opened the door to new types of criticism. A generation later, Martin Dibelius, Karl Ludwig Schmidt and other form critics took a stance directly opposed to the use of literary analysis as a tool of synoptic gospel criticism. Dibelius wrote:

> The literary understanding of the synoptics begins with the recognition that they are collections of materials. The composers are only to the smallest extent authors. They are principally collectors, vehicles of tradition, editors.[5]

In the same vein Karl Ludwig Schmidt wrote:

> But on the whole there is little life of Jesus in the sense of developing biography, little chronological development of the story of Jesus, but only isolated stories, pericopae, which have been put in a framework.[6]

Reaction against the form critical method brought about renewed interest in the gospels as complete documents and in their literary qualities. Redaction critics undertook to examine the distinctive characteristics of each synoptic writer and the unifying force of those characteristics on the structure of the gospel.

The redaction critics raised many problems about the nature of the gospels.[7] Some of these questions carry researchers back into the realms of tradition, source and historical criticism; some carry them forward into modern literary criticism. For example, a very significant question raised by redaction critics is the question of the nature of the gospels. Just what is a gospel?[8] The response to this question and to other similar concerns is seen as supplementary to the findings of other types of criticism. The literary critic begins with study of the completed text as does the redaction critic.

The expression literary criticism carries a variety of meanings and thus needs to be carefully defined. In its broadest sense, literary criticism can apply to the study of anything which is written. However, it had been more generally used, before the advent of modern critical approaches, for the study of a literary work by learning about the author, the time and place in which he lived, and his purpose for writing if this were known. Today the focus of literary criticism is on analysis and appreciation of the text. Even this narrower sense of literary criticism carries at least two meanings. It is used for the study of the formal, thematic and stylistic aspects of any writing which is not specifically involved in imparting knowledge. This type of literary criticism concerns itself with the study of drama, essays, poems, novels—the material found in "literature" texts. This literary critic may view the text as having instrumental value *or* as having its end in itself.

But in a narrower sense, literary criticism concerns itself with the elements of a text which delight or instruct the reader in themselves. The literary critic examines a text in order to derive from it knowledge of plot, character, language and style, diction and other qualities of the writing itself. This critic sees form as an essential element of the meaning, not as an instrument of meaning. This literary critic views the text as having final rather than instrumental value.

When used of biblical study, the expression literary criticism is again multidimensional. It had been used in earlier critical studies for the examination of such external characteristics as author, date, place, assumed purpose. In more recent studies, literary criticism of the Bible has centered upon content in relation to form, upon the capacities of language, upon the role of genre in determining meaning: "More recently, however, biblical authors have been paying attention to the criticism of fiction and poetry and to aesthetics and philosophy of language."[9] Nonetheless, even here there are two dimensions. The expression literary criticism can be used for the study of an over-all sense which includes rhetorical criticism, that is, the devices employed in order to persuade, or it can be used to indicate something separate from rhetorical criticism, that is, the structures and meanings in themselves. In this study the expression literary criticism will be used to include specifically rhetorical elements as well as other literary devices.

Rhetorical criticism is a comparatively new method in biblical research. William Beardslee, basing his discussion on the Aristotelian distinction between rhetoric and poetic, summarizes the origin of the rhetorical approach to New Testament studies. He writes:

> Since persuasion was the aim of ancient rhetoric, and since persuasion has also been an important aim not only for the New Testament writers but for those who have studied them in later times, it is not surprising that many of the approaches to literary study of the New Testament have been in terms of this type of analysis.[10]

Rhetorical criticism has emphases of its own and the specific difference from poetic criticism is that it studies the means used to induce knowledge, assent, acceptance. Rhetorical criticism views discourse as an instrument in a speech process. The tone of such discourse is personal because author and reader are implicated in the process.

A modern practitioner and theoretician of rhetorical criticism, George Kennedy, regards it as "an additional tool of interpretation to complement form criticism, redaction criticism, historical and literary criticism."[11] Types of criticism often overlap and frequently operate out of the same basic presuppositions. Therefore it is important to see the relationship of this additional tool to the other critical approaches. For the purpose of this study, in common with redactional critical method, the matter for analysis is the final text of Mark's gospel.[12] Literary critics and rhetorical critics use the same method of approach to the text; however, rhetorical criticism has as its purpose to decipher the message of the text through study of the literary and rhetorical means used to achieve it. It assumes, therefore, that the form of the narrative is instrumental to the message in distinction from literary criticism which sees the text as having final value in itself.

Kennedy makes a necessary further distinction between his type of literary-rhetorical criticism and that employed by Northrop Frye in *The Great Code;* Frye brings to bear upon the New Testament texts all of the equipment available to the twentieth century scholar: the study of typology, of types of authorship, of translational problems, of oratorical traditions, of myth and metaphor, all as understood by scholars long after the completion of the New Testament. Frye writes:

> The relating of one's "literal" understanding of the Bible as a book to the rest of one's knowledge, more particularly to the Bible's "background" in history and culture, thus creates a synthesis that begins to move from the level of knowledge and understanding to an existential level, from Dante's "allegorical" to his "tropological" meaning, from Kierkegaard's "either" to his "or".[13]

Kennedy proposes to take a more direct approach to the text by concentrating on the elements which constitute its rhetoric, that is, its power of persuasion, those elements by which the author seeks to accomplish some purpose, as much as possible prescinding from modern interpretive insights. This is the understanding of rhetorical criticism which forms the background for this work.

Those who employ the rhetorical critical method find forerunners of that method in scholars who never heard the phrase applied to the study of the Bible. The basic distinction, of course, had come from Aristotle.[14] In *The History of the Synoptic Tradition,* Rudolph Bultmann offered what might be considered a preamble to rhetorical criticism by listing seven characteristics of story telling in the synoptic gospels. He enumerates: conciseness, scenic duality, heightened differentiation and individualization, minimal use of motives and feelings, indirect speech made direct, repetition, doublets and triplets.[15] All in some measure are literary characteristics and the matter of literary criticism. Some contribute directly to the rhetorical patterns. There are difficulties with Bultmann's classifications but scholarship such as his helped to move critical efforts in the direction of the concerns that rhetorical criticism makes its own.

The name and the method of rhetorical criticism were offered as a challenge to the world of biblical scholarship by James Muilenberg in his presidential address to the Society of Biblical Literature on December 18, 1968. This address, which was later published as an essay, gives the name to rhetorical criticism and explains that the major concerns of the rhetorical critic are:

> to observe the formal rhetorical devices which are employed, but more important, the substance or content of these most strategic loci, and to recognize the structure of a composition and to discern the configuration of its component parts, to delineate the warp and woof out of which the literary fabric is woven, and to note the various rhetorical devices that are employed.[16]

Rhetorical devices are almost as numerous as the writings which can be classified as rhetorical. Anything which contributes to the meaning and impact of a text is rhetorical. Rhetorical devices can be as simple as choice of vocabulary and as complex as parallelism. Rhetorical criticism can concern itself with study of small structures such as words and phrases or with the over-all structure of an entire narrative. The purpose is always to achieve a better understanding of the text.

Rhetorical criticism is a new discipline and has, happily, not settled into a specific methodology. The present work begins with the completed text of Mark's gospel. It employs the tools of literary and more specifically of rhetorical analysis. It looks to the text itself and to the literary and rhetorical devices used therein in order to discern patterns of meaning. It is not an attempt to do rhetorical criticism as that discipline is employed in contemporary biblical study just as it is not redaction criticism. It is an attempt to do a holistic reading of Mark which is related to redaction criticism and uses the devices of rhetorical and literary criticism.

The Order of the Synoptic Gospels

Basic to this study is the assumption that Mark's gospel is a literary document. To say that it is a narrative is to assume that Mark was an author with all the prerogatives of author, properly so called. The question of the genre of the gospels has produced a great deal of writing.[17] Mark's gospel has produced its own volume of material.[18] Before discussing the problem of the genre of Mark, and because the nature of this study requires comparison of synoptic texts, some positioning in regard to the order of the synoptics is in order.

Assumptions and conclusions about the order of the synoptic gospels have been diverse and contradictory.[19] For example, one scholar, G.M. Styler, "proves" that Mark was the first of the synoptic gospels to have been written. Another, W.R. Farmer, "proves" that Mark was last. Since both positions can be supported by cogent evidence, it seems impossible to take a firm position in favor of the priority of any one of the synoptics. It seems valid, therefore, to assume that the Markan author had the opportunity to select and to choose both his basic materials and the details with which he enhanced, or failed to enhance them.

Stemming from the question of priority is the further question about Mark's use of sources. This question of how much knowledge Mark had of other source materials has long been debated. Simply stated the problem is this: either the sayings material in Matthew and Luke is entirely made up or it comes from some source or sources. Since almost no one accepts the first possibility, there very probably were sources which predated Matthew and Luke. If such existed, either Mark knew them or he did not. It seems all but impossible that he would not have known them since that would require that he had been very isolated. Furthermore, Mark alludes to materials not found in Matthew and Luke, for example in the teaching sections (4:33 and 10:1) and in the summaries (6:56 and 3:7–12). Thus, it seems safe to assume that Mark had access to written and oral sources and that he selected and edited what he wished to use from these sources. It may also be assumed that he omitted or added to pericopae just as Matthew and Luke may be seen to have done so. For example, Luke includes the story of the raising of the son of the widow of Naim (7:11–17) and the parable of the good Samaritan (10:30–35). Neither Matthew nor Mark has these pericopae. Only Matthew includes the explanation of the parable of the weeds (13:36–42) and the parable of the unforgiving servant (18:23–35). Obviously, Matthew and Luke used sources other than Mark and added and deleted material when they wished. This adds cogency to the argument that Mark, too, knew and used both written and oral sources.

If one accepts the priority of Mark, this in no way deprives Mark of the prerogatives of a true author: in fact, it supports the contention. Assuming that the evidence of the text refutes the positions taken by Dibelius and Schmidt,[20] it is consistent with the above to assert that Mark fashioned the materials of his gospel according to his own presuppositions. If one were to contend that Matthew was first, the question is only slightly more problematic. It is obvious that Mark differs significantly from Matthew and Luke. To assume that this was the last of the synoptic gospels to have been written could certainly be seen as evidence of true authorship, that is, of a role in selecting, omitting, formulating, conflating and organizing the oral and possibly the written accounts. The brevity of the Markan account, though, has often been utilized as proof of its priority. Nevertheless, the same brevity could be used to support the proposition that Mark was a very selective and judicious author and that he conflated the Matthean and Lukan narratives. So, a valid position in regard to the order of the synoptic gospels seems to be that they all employed such a complex of source materials that no hypothesis about priority or order can be substantiated.

Since our knowledge of the predecessors of the extant gospels is severely limited, it might well have been that the Lukan author reflected the actual situation when he introduced his gospel with the words: "Inasmuch as many have undertaken to compile a narrative of the things which have been accomplished among us . . . " (Luke 1:1). It is, therefore, an assumption of this study that Mark, along with Matthew and Luke, chose the materials he wished to use from among existing sources and fashioned them in accordance with his literary and theological presuppositions. Thus it may be assumed that Mark omitted or added to pericopae, just as Matthew and Luke seem to have done. Mark was, therefore, an author in the fullest sense of the word.

The Gospel of Mark as Narrative

To describe a writing as narrative does not require that one deny the origin of its parts or that it is made up of originally distinct parts. It requires only that one demonstrate that its parts have been woven into an artistic unity. Many scholars have proved to their own satisfaction that Mark's gospel is a narrative. Others have simply assumed that it is and have worked from that assumption.

Those who have chosen to prove the contention have based their conclusions about the narrative nature of Mark's gospel on differing evidences. For example:

The narrative character of the gospel genre has been realized long ago ... the most striking characteristic of the gospel genre is "point of view" ... in short, he creates a narrative world with its own set of characters, intertextual net of references, space and time.[21]

The study of Mark as narrative reveals more unity and art in the gospel than is commonly recognized. These appear as we consider the narrative lines which flow from the commissions or tasks of major characters in the gospel ... among the compositional techniques considered in this study were the delayed disclosure of Jesus' and the disciples' full commissions, and the repeated use of irony, paradox and enticement to falsehood.[22]

It is clear that the narrator's subjective knowledge of his characters' thoughts and feelings pervades his narrative ... the rhetorical consistency of his own narrative is nothing short of remarkable.[23]

A second group of critics has simply assumed the narrative character of Mark's gospel. David Rhoads and Donald Michie analyze quite thoroughly the narrative patterns and devices in the story. At no point do they undertake to prove the underlying hypothesis.[24] Robert M. Fowler builds a discussion of the Markan feeding stories around the nature of their composition and concludes that only by means of literary criticism can the mystery of the two feeding stories be solved:

To answer the question of why an author would rewrite a traditional story, place his new composition two chapters before the old story, and allow a certain problematic tension to exist between these stories, we found it necessary to consult literary critics.[25]

Donald Juel writes: "We should begin with the assumption that Mark was at least capable of telling a coherent story, that there is a certain structure and cohesiveness to his gospel."[26]

Joanna Dewey does not mention the underlying assumption of narrative status but the cogency of her argument about the concentric structures in Mark buttresses such a conclusion.[27]

This study employs the second of the two paths. It is assumed that Mark's gospel is a narrative. It has a unified and connected plot which revolves around the central character Jesus, and, as will be shown, it has a unifying theme. The discussion centers on two levels of meaning and the irony which sometimes results from that duality. The duality is seen throughout the gospel as a unifying element and is a factor contributing to the narrative nature of the gospel. The insight that Erich Auerbach brought to bear on the New Testament writings is relevant. Their "sensory occurrence pales before the power of the figural meaning."[28] The word used is "pales," not disappears. The narrative line is there and narrative devices of point of view, plot, character and setting are there. This narrative line must be seen as having two levels of meaning, however.

As it is used here the word "level" refers to a plane of meaning. Throughout this study the expression "level of meaning" is to be understood as a description of a meaning structure which is complete in itself and can be seen as indissolubly related to another such plane of meaning but separable from it. The expression "level of meaning" can be explained in a series of literary examples. For example, words have meanings simultaneously on more than one level of reference. Literary analysts distinguish several levels of reference for each word:

> It has a restricted definition or core meaning known as its denotation. It may have implied associations, known as its connotation. Finally, it may function as an allusion, which is an indirect reference to another word or idea of greater meaning.
> Example: Sunday
> Denotation: the first day of the week

Connotation: a day of worship
Allusion: Hypocritical (as in a "Sunday Christian")[29]

Another example can be found in the use of symbolism, for example,

> More generally, Paul Elmer Moore has indicated that all symbols fall into one of four levels (each including all below it); (1) significative: the arbitrary, conventional sign (often with all emotion removed): H_2O; r^2; "rally round the flag." (2) metaphoric: the first, plus a natural association still felt: "pure as the lily." (3) commemorative: adds the recollection of a literal occasion: "For each man has his cross to bear." (4) sacramental: the symbol is the thing symbolized: "to eat of the bread."[30]

The expression "level of meaning" is used in this study to signify a plane of meaning, which, in terms of form, is similar to that of allegory.

> Allegory-Rh. A trope in which a second meaning is to be read beneath and concurrent with the surface story.[31]

In an allegory two levels or planes of meaning run concurrently from beginning to end. Mark's gospel possesses two levels of meaning which run from beginning to end but are decidedly not formative of an allegory because neither level is metaphorical. One plane of the meaning structure of Mark's gospel is devoted to a proclamatory portrayal of Jesus as Messiah and Son of God at the same time that, on another complete plane of meaning, he is described as a failure. This is close to the conclusion reached by Kermode that what is actually present in Mark is "the antithesis of silence and proclamation,"[32] but, instead of silence, it is more accurate to understand a pole of failure to believe or to understand.

Mark as Biography

It is important to note that Mark's gospel, in common with Matthew's and Luke's, has significant parallels to biography, at least as that genre was understood in the ancient world. Early in the present century, the question of the nature of the gospels as biography had been raised:

> Biographies of the Greek and Roman intellectual leaders were written primarily to exhibit and perpetuate their teaching. The major portion of the material is quotation of their words and the main interest centers in their ideas. . . . Among the biographical writings of the ancient Greek literature, the nearest parallels to the Gospels are the books which report the lives of Epictetus, Apollonius and Socrates.[33]

Charles Talbert has investigated the biographical elements of each of the gospels and has somewhat questionably concluded that

> Mark is a Type B biography of Jesus. It was written to defend against a misunderstanding of the church's savior and to portray a true image of him for the disciples to follow. This gospel was written in terms of the myth of the immortals. This gives the story of Jesus its overall structure and indicates that the gospel functioned as a myth of origins for an early Christian community.[34]

Talbert's method for developing his thesis is to refute the criteria discerned by Bultmann for determining if any gospel fits the ancient concept of biography. Bultmann concludes that Graeco-Roman biographies did not deal with mythic and cultic matters and, since the gospels do, the gospels do not fit the pattern of Graeco-Roman biography. Talbert contends that ancient biography did, indeed, concern itself with cultic and mythic functions and attitudes and that, therefore, the gospels

fit the pattern. His conclusion is, of course, totally contrary to
Bultmann's. There is some difficulty with Talbert's system of
classification since he describes five types of ancient biography
without examples or documentation to support his conclusions. This weakens the validity of his arguments. Nonetheless, he correctly directs attention to the biographical elements
of this gospel.

The same weakness does not appear in Philip Shuler's
attempt to define the relationship between ancient biography
and the gospels. In *A Genre for the Gospels,* Shuler examines
Graeco-Roman *bios* literature. From this fairly extensive
examination he derives a description of the laudatory biography, or *encomium.* Shuler examines Matthew's gospel as an
example of the *encomium* and finds many correspondences
with the ancient form. To this point Shuler's argument seems
sound, but in his concluding remarks he writes, "One can
hardly deny to Mark, Luke and John, for example, Matthew's
focus on the *bios* of Jesus."[35] The conclusion seems to outstrip
the evidence there and again when he adds:

> Furthermore, even a cursory reading of these three gos-
> pels suggests that the biographical patterns employ *topoi,*
> techniques and purposes similar to those employed in
> *encomium* biography.[36]

It is precisely the study of Shuler's claim that leads to careful
examination of those elements of the biography which
unquestionably are found in Mark's gospel. Such examination,
far from supporting a claim that Mark's gospel is an *encomium* biography, calls it into serious question.

These and other discussions of the gospels as biographies
have added to the recognition of the role of biographical elements in the gospel. However, other aspects of Mark's gospel
preclude the possibility of understanding it, simply or wholly,
as biography. The rhetoric is directed toward other perspec-

tives of Jesus' life, such as proclamations and negations, which cannot be contained within the definition of biography.

NOTES

[1] William Wrede, *Das Messiasgeheimnis in den Evangelien* (Göttingen: Vandenhoeck and Ruprecht, 1901).

[2] See, for example, James Moffat, *An Introduction to the New Testament* (Edinburgh: T and T Clark, 1928).

[3] By 1974, *Semeia,* an experimental journal for biblical criticism, had appeared. *Semeia* (Decatur: SBL Press, 1974–1988).

[4] See discussion in Joachim Gnilka, *Das Evangelium nach Markus* (Zürich: Benzinger Verlag, Auflage 1978), p. 167, for example.

[5] Martin Dibelius, *From Tradition to Gospel* trans. B.L. Woolf (London: Nicholson and Watson, 1934), p. 3.

[6] Karl Ludwig Schmidt, *Der Rahmen der Geschichte Jesus* (Darmstadt: Wissenchaftliche Buchgesellschaft, 1969), p. 317 (trans. mine).

[7] An excellent explanation of the manner in which redaction criticism reached its point of prominence can be found in Norman Perrin's *What Is Redaction Criticism?* (Philadelphia: Fortress, 1969).

[8] Charles H. Talbert, *What Is a Gospel?* (London: SPCK, 1978), et al.

[9] William A. Beardslee, *Literary Criticism of the New Testament* (Philadelphia: Fortress, 1970), p. iii.

[10] Beardslee, *Literary Criticism,* p. 3.

[11] George A. Kennedy, *New Testament Interpretation through Rhetorical Criticism* (Chapel Hill: University of North Carolina, 1984), p. 3.

[12] All references to the final text of Mark's gospel are to Nestle-Aland, *Novum Testamentum Graece* (Stuttgart: Deutsche Bibilstiftung, 1979). All quotations in English are from the *Revised Standard Version* or are the author's own translation.

[13] Northrop Frye, *The Great Code: The Bible and Literature* (Toronto: Academic Press, 1981), pp. 228–229.

[14] Aristotle, *On Poetry* (Indianapolis: Bobbs-Merrill, 1956). *The Art of Rhetoric*, Eng. trans. J.H. Freese, vol. 22, Loeb Classical Library (Cambridge: Harvard University Press, 1947).

[15] Rudolf Bultmann, *The History of the Synoptic Tradition*, trans. John March, rev. ed. (New York: Harper and Row, 1968), pp. 307–317.

[16] James Muilenberg, "Form Criticism and Beyond," *Journal of Biblical Literature* 88 (1969), 1–18, pp. 9–10.

[17] For example, David L. Barr, *Toward a Definition of a Gospel Genre* (Florida State University, Ph.D. dissertation, 1974). Talbert, *What Is A Gospel?* Philip L. Shuler, *A Genre for the Gospels* (Philadelphia: Fortress, 1982).

[18] Joanna Dewey, *Markan Public Debate* (Chico: Society of Biblical Literature, 1980). Ernest Best, *Mark: The Gospel as Story* (Edinburgh: T and T Clark, 1983), et al.

[19] See G.M. Styler, "The Priority of Mark," in C.F.D. Moule, *The Birth of the New Testament* (San Francisco: Harper and Row, 1982). William R. Farmer, *The Synoptic Problem* (New York: Macmillan, 1964), et al.

[20] See above, Foreword.

[21] W.S. Vorster, "Kerygma/History and the Gospel Genre," *New Testament Studies* 29 (1983), 91.

[22] Robert C. Tannehill, "The Gospel of Mark as Narrative Christology," *Semeia* 13 (1979), 88–89.

[23] Norman R. Peterson, "Point of View in Mark's Narrative," *Semeia* 12 (1978), 118.

[24] David Rhoads and Donald Michie, *Mark as Story* (Philadelphia: Fortress, 1982).

[25] Robert M. Fowler, *Loaves and Fishes* (Chico: Scholars Press, 1981), p. 182.

[26] Donald Juel, *Messiah and Temple* (Missoula: Scholars Press, 1977), p. 6.

[27] Joanna Dewey, *Markan Public Debate.*

[28] Erich Auerbach, *Mimesis* (New York: Doubleday, 1953), p. 43.

[29] Harry Brown and John Milstead, *Patterns in Poetry* (Glenview, Illinois: Scott, Foresman, 1968), p. 136.

[30] Joseph T. Shipley, *Dictionary of World Literature* (Totowa, New Jersey: Littlefield Adams, 1953), pp. 408–409.

[31] Shipley, *Dictionary,* p. 13.

[32] Frank Kermode, *The Genesis of Secrecy* (Cambridge: Harvard University Press, 1979), p. 140.

[33] Clyde Weber Votaw, *The Gospels and Contemporary Biographies in the Graeco-Roman World,* reprint ed. (Philadelphia: Fortress, 1970), pp. 9–10.

[34] Talbert, *What Is a Gospel?* p. 134.

[35] Philip L. Shuler, *A Genre for the Gospels,* p. 109.

[36] Ibid.

Chapter 2

PROBLEM AND METHOD

· · · _____ · · ·

The Problem

The use of repetition, parallelism, antithetical structures and dual meanings in Mark's gospel has been noted by many scholars. These devices are so frequent and so important that they almost constitute a pattern of narrative technique. Frank Kermode used the term "structural oppositions" to describe the device of bringing together significantly antithetical persons, actions or words.[1] Frans Neirynck wrote about dual meanings in Mark that

> on the whole, the evidence (for duplicate expressions) is rather impressive, especially the fact that a kind of general tendency can be perceived in vocabulary and grammar, in individual sayings, in the construction of pericopes and larger sections; there is a sort of homogeneity in Mark, from the wording of sentences to the composition of the gospel.[2]

The "general tendency" of which Neirynck speaks may be a pattern of narrative technique which tends to function on two levels of meaning in words, incidents and the entire narrative. Many studies propose examples of two levels of meaning used in the Markan narrative. David Rhoads lists authors whose works center on dual structures which form strong motifs in the Markan narrative. He lists Neirynck, Thomas E. Boomershine, Howard Clark Kee, William Telford, Joanna Dewey, Donald Juel and Robert Fowler.[3]

Jack Dean Kingsbury writes that "there are two major aspects to Mark's portrait of Jesus."[4] He compares Mark's portrayal of Jesus as Son of God with Jesus' self-identification as Son of Man. He views these dual aspects of the portrait as complementary, not as contrasting.

In *About the Gospels,* C.H. Dodd wrote, "The total effect of these passages (in Mark), and many others like them, is to suggest a mysterious undercurrent beneath the ostensible."[5] He later adds that "Mark is perfectly aware of this undercurrent of mystery in his story."[6] Dodd perceives a story of Jesus' martyrdom and an additional level of meaning which is much deeper.

Vernon K. Robbins has published a study of socio-rhetorical forms in Mark's gospel. Two of these forms he distinguishes as "progressive" and "repetitive." The progressive forms may be logical or qualitative and, he says, it is these that build the argumentation. He adds that there are two theses within the narrative argumentation in Mark's gospel, "one concerning the Messiah and another concerning Kingship."[7] Robbins pursues this argument to the conclusion that the reader must understand the life of Jesus on two different levels. He must comprehend the suffering and death of Jesus as an historic reality which occurred in ancient Palestine. At the same time, the reader is called to realize their meaning within the culture and society of his own time.[8] Once again there are two levels of meaning being developed.

Scholarship seems to be moving in the direction of close attention to the dual nature of the narrative in Mark. However, there seems to be a reticence, even a hesitation, to face squarely the decidedly negative aspects of that gospel and to understand the gospel in the light of those negations.

Norman R. Petersen can be said to demonstrate this type of hesitation:

The prism of Mark 16:8, literally understood, leads to a total revision, indeed to a hermeneutical inversion, of all expectations and satisfactions generated prior to it. None of them any longer mean what, until 16:8, we thought they meant. Throughout the narrative, Jesus has been depicted to us as a reliable character who purposefully goes about his business encumbered only by the lagging intellects of his chosen twelve.[9]

Then he goes on to be sure it all turns out all right:

First, the reader recognizes irony in 16:8 because a literal reading of it makes nonsense of the narrator's previous generation of expectations and satisfactions being enjoyed as recently as 16:6 where the young man announces, "he has risen."[10]

The assumption which underlies Petersen's argument about the ironic nature of the final verse of Mark, an argument that has to be taken seriously, is that everything which precedes 16:8 is consistently leading the reader to expect something other than this abrupt ending. By his assertion that a literal reading of 16:8 makes "nonsense of the narrator's previous generation of expectations and satisfactions," Petersen is assuming a single orientation. He misses the dual orientation which is basic to Mark's gospel. Far from being a total inversion of all of the expectations generated by the gospel, 16:8 is totally consonant with one of the two levels of understanding upon which Mark must be read. There is a level of understanding which proclaims that Jesus is the Christ, the Son of God. There is a second level of understanding which reflects not just the inability of the disciples to understand, but the total rejection of Jesus by his family and neighbors and by official Judaism, the failure of his disciples, even the change in the ubiquitous crowd who had followed him so ardently. This duality permeates the entire gospel. It results in a level of affirmation where Jesus is unequivocally known as Messiah and Son of God and in a level of negation where human seeing, hearing, perceiving and understanding are not enough to make Jesus successful.

In considering laudatory and non-laudatory, positive and negative elements of such an ancient portrait, it must be assumed that, even in an intensely laudatory presentation of a hero, there must be found some negative elements. There might well be those who are openly hostile, those who raise serious objections, those who defect. If the story is to have vitality and tension, there must be some opposition, some failure. On the other hand, in the first century the laudatory biography had some specific characteristics:

> As the educated of that time (the time of Philostratus) well knew, Aristotle had defined an *encomium* as having one purpose: to praise the achievements of the person in question, beginning with "noble birth and education ... virtuous parents (and) all attendant circumstances" (Rhetoric I. ix.33). A record of noble achievements reveals that man's noble character. Therefore the encomiast's duty is to stress these to the complete exclusion of everything else—especially questionable or derogatory events or traits.
>
> We may therefore surmise in the case of Philostratus what we know is true of Philo, that any negative or objectionable aspects were intentionally glossed over or carefully explained so as to appear in a favorable light.[11]

A distinction needs to be made at this point because the *encomium* always uses hostile forces, obstacles, misunderstandings, as necessary background to achieve dramatic effect. With great regularity these negative backdrops are converted into positive supports. Otherwise, they are totally vanquished.

In the *Life of Apollonios of Tyana* by Philostratus, for example, seven of Apollonios' disciples refuse to accompany him on his first trip to India and on subsequent journeys.[12] He fails to convert the Egyptians to his philosophy.[13] His final trial before Domitian would have ended in execution, had he not miraculously disappeared.[14] In one of the accounts of his final days on earth, he was arrested and jailed as a wizard and a thief.[15]

In each of these examples it is easy to detect an intent to enhance the stature of Apollonios rather than to negate it. The desertion of Apollonios by his disciples, used several times, stresses the bravery and purposefulness of the hero in spite of these defections. His failure to convince the Egyptians of his philosophy is caused by the evil machinations of a sinister rival, the philosopher Euphrates. This device creates dramatic tension. The author finally loses interest in this conflict and allows it to dissolve into a geographical excursus (Book VI). The details of Apollonios' trial before Domitian heighten the dramatic tension in order to stress the stature of Apollonios: for example, in his Socratic-like self-defense in VIII. 8–9. The use of three accounts of the death of Apollonios perhaps indicates the author's inability to control his intense desire to praise the hero. The negative details in these incidents are used to accentuate his heroism; for example, the imprisonment is ended by his deliberately freeing himself in order to enter heaven (VIII. 30).

Another example can be found in Philo's "Life of Moses."[16] The extravagances of the description of Moses' early years, even to the anachronism that he was taught by Greek philosophers, are always held in dramatic tension with the description of his Hebrew heritage. Moses is somehow understood to be the grandson of the Egyptian king, at the same time as he "remained loyal to his own ancient, native culture" (I. 32). Moses' action in killing the evil taskmaster is exonerated ("justifying his action as the right thing to do," I. 44). Moses' mistake in leading the Hebrews to a dead-end by the Red Sea is portrayed by Philo as a deliberate test of Moses' obedience. The incidents which Philo chose to omit from his biblical source are instructive. He has no description of Aaron's leadership in the construction of the golden calf and he does not mention Moses' exclusion from the promised land

and the reason for it. Philo soars to the heights of praise in Book II where Moses is portrayed as law-giver, high priest and prophet. His final triumph occurs when, rising into heaven, he "prophesied shrewdly concerning his own death" (II. 291). Philo employs opposition and conflict in the service of dramatic tension.

The use of negative factors to produce dramatic tension is obviously necessary even in the most laudatory of presentations. However, important differences exist between such use of negations and the Markan usage.

    a.   In the Markan narration, negative elements are so consistent and pervasive that they form a distinct level of meaning. Nothing even close to this occurs in the *encomia*.

    b.   In the Markan account, many devices are used to emphasize those who fail to understand, or do not believe, or do not act with courage. In the *encomia*, attention is focused on the failures as a literary device to enhance the stature of the hero by contrast.

    c.   Mark uses negative elements to produce dramatic tension as the *encomiasts* do. However, he adds a further negative portrayal, many negative results and relationships which go far beyond the necessities of drama.

    d.   Mark does not resolve the arguments, hostilities, failures at the end of his gospel, as the *encomiasts* do.

Thus, the Markan usage of negatives shares many characteristics with the dramatic tension found in any biographical writing but is also essentially different from it.

Sometimes the Markan author chose to use the negative elements for purposes other than negation. For example, the disagreements with scribes and Pharisees over practices of oral law (7:1–13 et al.) called for an evaluation of some of these practices. The desensationalizing of some miracle stories helped to place them in their proper perspective as demonstrations of the ways of God with men rather than as occasions for semi-hysterical enthusiasm. It will be important to distinguish outcomes of negative usages which support the affirmative level of meaning from those which support the negative level.

It is even more important to note that duality can bring about a contrast between the level of understanding shared by both the narrator and reader, who always know that Jesus is Messiah and Son of God, and that of the characters in the story, who do not know who he is. This seems to permit a type of dramatic irony which manifests itself throughout the narrative as proclamations of who Jesus is are placed in juxtaposition with statements of unbelief and misunderstanding. The same ironic contrast can be found in situations where Jesus has acted as Son of God and been misunderstood for it:

> There is certainly a distinction to be made between a situation in which a man does not fully understand the meaning of the words he uses or hears and one in which he does not fully understand the situation he is in, but both are forms of dramatic irony.[17]

The type of irony which is found in Mark's gospel has been discussed in some detail by modern students of the gospel. Dan Via has pointed out that

> the irony in the course of events victimizes the protagonist and brings him to the stature of a tragic hero. The opposition to Jesus culminating in his death ironically brings him to victory while his opponents' apparent victory causes their defeat.[18]

Donald Juel develops the point that irony is involved in the mockery of Jesus as prophet (14:65) at the very moment that his prophecy is being fulfilled (14:66–72).[19] Wayne Booth also directs attention to the function of irony in the Markan gospel. His concern is with the response of the reader to an ironic passage:

> But the ironic form can be shared by everyone who has
> any sympathy for Jesus at all, man or God: even the reader
> who sees him as a self-deluded fanatic is likely to join
> Mark in his reading of the irony, and thus to have his
> sympathy for the crucified man somewhat increased.[20]

Robert Fowler concludes: "The readers of Mark find most of his irony easily comprehensible, so much so, in fact, that there has been too little explicit recognition of it," and further that "the Messianic Secret is a rhetorical device, the use of irony to narrate the 'gospel of Jesus Christ, the Son of God.'"[21]

The dramatic irony which seems to be operative in Mark's gospel occurs when the reader knows who Jesus is and the characters in the narrative do not know this. It also seems operative when the author leads the reader to compare the actions and words of characters in the drama to knowledge and understandings which the reader already possesses. The thesis of a dual structure permits the hypothesis that dramatic irony is one important rhetorical device used in Mark's gospel from the proclamation of 1:1, "The beginning of the gospel of Jesus Christ, the Son of God," to the moment the women run off and fail to deliver the message, "for they were afraid" (16:8).

It is the purpose of this work to prove that a basic level of negation exists in the Markan narrative. This level of negation is at least as important to the literary structure as the level of affirmation. The level of affirmation, of accepting the various proclamations of the gospel, has been recognized for twenty centuries. During all of that time, it overrode the negative. As early as Origen we read, "The Word Himself and the Truth Himself might be saying to the confessor and to the denier: 'The measure you give will be the measure you get back'" (Luke 6:38; Matthew 7:2; Mark 4:24).[22] Similarly, he writes, "This threefold wrestling is written in the three gospels (Mt. 4:1–11; Lk. 4:1–13; Mk. 1:12–13), where our Savior as man is understood to have conquered the enemy three times."[23] And John Chrysostom comments on Mark 6:8 and parallels, "I shall furnish proof of Christ's power: I shall show that Christ is God."[24]

More recent scholarship follows the pattern of subsuming the negative elements within the affirmative ones. Early in the present century Julius Wellhausen wrote:

> Mark did not write "de vita et moribus Jesu." He has no intention of making Jesus' person manifest, or even intelligible. For him it has been absorbed in Jesus' divine vocation. He wishes to demonstrate that Jesus is the Christ.[25]

The trend continues even with the most recent studies which have restored Mark to its proper place as an important early church document but have continued to conclude that it ends affirmatively. A few examples from among many:

> In Mark's interpretation, then, the life of Jesus, despite its outward show of tragic frustration, is really a continuous fulfillment of God's plan of salvation.[26]

> Thus rather than being an ending with unaccepted negative overtones, Mark 16:7, 8 constitutes a positive and glorious affirmation not only of the resurrection of the Christ but of his continued presence in the Christian community in the power of his word.[27]

> The end of Jesus' life stands at the heart of the gospel: the historical Jesus like the kerygmatic Christ is the crucified Messiah.[28]

> The effect of the ending could be called a purging of the fear associated with the apostolic commission. Thus, the ending is a climactic reversal of expectations in the central Marcan motif of the messianic secret.[29]

> Mark sees the historical Jesus and the preached Christ as one and the same; therefore he retells the events of the

earthly life of Jesus at the same time as he presents him through these as son of God and son of man.[30]

The trend continues until our own day. As recently as 1985, Vernon K. Robbins wrote:

> For them (the early Christians) the promises of God reached their fulfillment in a social and cultural framework of understanding that required suffering and rejection as a way of identity and integrity until the Son of Man would come in the glory of the Father with the holy angels.[31]

This final sentence of Robbins' study of the socio-rhetorical forms in Mark's gospel carefully subsumes the negative elements of rejection and suffering into the proclamation of the coming in glory. After studying repetitive and progressive forms and the teacher-disciple relationship, Robbins concludes that there are negative elements. He writes: "No one in the document fully responds to the persuasive manifestation of the system enacted by Jesus,"[32] and, "In contrast (to readers of Xenophon's *Memorabilia*) the reader of Mark is left with the fear and flight of the women in addition to the fear and flight of the disciples."[33] Negative conclusions such as these are consistently balanced by analyses of Jesus' role as Son of God in full possession of authority and wisdom. Robbins' work demonstrates a common procedure for treatment of negative elements in Mark's gospel.

The procedure of subsuming the negative elements of the gospel under the affirmative has been so obvious down through the centuries that no one could seriously attempt to discredit it. However, the negative level has not been allowed to carry the weight it actually bears within the text. Scholars have been reluctant to allow the full weight of the negations to assume their proper significance within a negative level.

It is a working hypothesis of this study that a particular type of dramatic irony is made possible by the dual aspects of

the portrait of Jesus. In many ironies it is the chief character
who does not know what the audience knows. In Mark's gospel, the chief character, Jesus, knows who he is (1:10–11; 2:24
etc.). It is the characters who surround Jesus who do not recognize who he is. The reader can surmise that at some point
they came to understand Jesus or the text would not exist, but
no such reversal of the ignorance occurs in the text.

In addition to the decisively negative aspects of the Markan gospel, there is also a general pattern of muting or neutralizing the positive effects of some incidents. These negative
elements require investigation. When the women run from the
tomb and from the young man's proclamation, and "tell no
one for they were afraid" (16:8), a final, decisive negation has
occurred. It is not rescinded, as the lack of understanding of
the disciples is not rescinded, as the lack of faith of Jesus' family is not rescinded, as the unfounded opposition of the Jewish
officials is not rescinded.

Mark's gospel can no longer be relegated to the status of
a primitive, loosely structured document, let alone one torn
asunder by "clumsy construction."[34] There are, indeed, some
less than artistic passages, but they do not dominate in this
writing. They are the kinds of awkwardnesses that are found
in most manuscripts. Even though there are a fair number of
such passages, it has lately been acknowledged that this gospel
is both literarily and theologically sophisticated.[35]

A constituent element of this finely wrought document is
the use of negation as one level of a duality wherein Jesus is
depicted as a total failure in the eyes of the other human
beings who appear in this story. At the same time, the narrator
and the reader know Jesus to be, albeit without proof, Son of
God and Messiah. There is no moment of recognition in the
Aristotelian sense and so the dramatic irony seems to endure
from the first verse to the last and to eventuate in ambiguity.
The negative elements in the portrayal of Jesus are totally consistent with the level of meaning on which Jesus was a failure.
Those who saw and heard him could have perceived and

understood, but they did not. The positive aspects of the portrayal function on a second level. Jesus is believed to be Messiah and Son of God. He is proclaimed such in confessional statements and there are some who come to him in faith. There is no human motivation for their coming in faith, nor for the proclamations. There is no human seeing, hearing, perceiving or even understanding which brings faith.

On the level of human failure, Jesus' family and friends and neighbors, disciples (the twelve and the special three or four), the crowds, Jewish officialdom, see, hear, sometimes perceive, rarely understand and never believe. On the level of proclamation, the narrator, the "voice," the unclean spirits, and finally the Roman centurion all know and believe. On this level there are no proofs offered; there is no human motivation for the belief of the narrator or of the Roman centurion, as there is none for the carriers of the paralytic, of Jairus, of the woman with hemorrhage, of the father of the demoniac, of Bartimaeus. Mark fully expects that the reader will know that the narrator's voice speaks that which is true and that he will also know that the level of failure results from misunderstanding and hardness of heart.

The Method

The proof of the statement that there is a level of negation in Mark's gospel, which pervades the whole and is neither subsumed nor explained away, involves two related tasks. The presentation of Jesus must be seen on the affirmative and on the negative levels. Then supporting evidence for the negative level must be presented, beginning with the most cogent evidence and ending with less certain possibilities. This evidence must be shown to constitute a complete level of meaning.

In pursuance of the first task, a Markan portrait of Jesus will be proposed. This portrait will be derived from the gospel in the same sequence as the original narrative. A level of affirmation will be described. This level indicates the nature of the proclamations of who Jesus is and how his actions demonstrate that. The level of negation will then be described in the same sequence. This level indicates how Jesus was misunderstood by many who should have understood and how some incidents are muted or neutralized in the narrative. This portrait, which will provide a sequential look at each of the two levels, is in fact a single portrait, the negative level of which needs to be taken seriously.

Following the portrait, evidence of the negative level of total meaning will be examined beginning with the most obvious and easily acceptable arguments and ending with evidence which can only be considered possible. Chief among the soundest arguments are the contrast with John the Baptizer and the study of the various groups who fail to understand Jesus. Evidence which is strong but less definitive than the preceding includes the enigma of the final pericope (16:8), the lack of resurrection narratives, the treatment of miracles, and the limiting of witnesses. Finally, some possible evidence will be provided in the discussion of the secrecy commands, of the role of the crowd, and of the passive portrayal of Jesus in key episodes.

There are stylistic devices which contribute to the negative portrayal either directly or by the process which will, herein, be called muting. The most obvious example of muting occurs when the narrator makes an important proclamation or statement and immediately directs attention away from it. The use of details in miracle stories is another such device. A third is the use of content-overload sentences which describe the who, when, where, what and how of an incident in rapid succession, thereby freeing the narrator to use the incident for his own purposes. Each of these devices will be examined in the pericopae in which they occur.

NOTES

[1] Frank Kermode, *The Genesis of Secrecy: On the Interpretation of Narrative,* p. 133.

[2] Frans Neirynck, *Duality in Mark* (Leuven: University Press, 1972), p. 37.

[3] David Rhoads, "Narrative Criticism and the Gospel of Mark," *Journal of the American Academy of Religion* 50 (1982): 424.

[4] Jack Dean Kingsbury, *The Christology of Mark* (Philadelphia: Fortress, 1983), p. 173.

[5] C.H. Dodd, *About the Gospels* (Cambridge: Cambridge University Press, 1950), p. 9.

[6] Ibid.

[7] Vernon K. Robbins, *Jesus the Teacher* (Philadelphia: Fortress, 1984), p. 201.

[8] Ibid. p. 213.

[9] Norman R. Petersen, "When Is the End Not an End?" *Interpretation* 34 (1980): 161.

[10] Ibid. p. 162.

[11] David R. Cartlidge and David L. Dungan, *Documents for the Study of the Gospels* (Philadelphia: Fortress, 1980), p. 256.

[12] Cartlidge *Documents* "Life of Apollonios of Tyana," I.18.

[13] Ibid. IV.1.

[14] Ibid. VIII.5.

[15] Ibid. VIII.8.

[16] Cartlidge, *Documents,* "Life of Moses," pp. 253–292.

[17] D.C. Muecke, *The Compass of Irony* (London: Methuen, 1969), p. 106.

[18] Dan O. Via, Jr., *Kerygma and Comedy in the New Testament* (Philadelphia: Fortress, 1975), p. 100.

[19] Juel, *Messiah and Temple,* p. 71.

[20] Wayne C. Booth, *A Rhetoric of Irony* (Chicago: University of Chicago Press, 1974), p. 29.

[21] Fowler, *Loaves,* pp. 98–99.

[22] Rowan A. Greer, *Origen* (New York: Paulist Press, 1979), p. 48.

[23] Ibid.

[24] Margaret A. Schatkin and P.W. Harkins, trans. and ed., *St. John Chrysostom: Apologist* (Washington: Catholic University Press, 1983), p. 189.

[25] Julius Wellhausen *Einleitung in die drei ersten Evangelien* (Berlin: George Reimer, 1905), p. 52 (trans. mine).

[26] T.A. Burkill, "Mysterious Revelation," in Christopher Tuckett, *The Messianic Secret* (Philadelphia: Fortress, 1983), p. 47.

[27] Robert P. Meye, *Jesus and the Twelve* (Grand Rapids: Eerdmans, 1968), pp. 218–219.

[28] Nils A. Dahl, *The Crucified Messiah and Other Essays* (Minneapolis: Augsburg Press, 1974), p. 34.

[29] Thomas E. Boomershine, "Mark 16:8 and the Apostolic Commission," *Journal of Biblical Literature* 100/2 (1981) 225–239: 238.

[30] Ernest Best, *Mark the Gospel as Story,* p. 139.

[31] Vernon K. Robbins, *Jesus the Teacher,* p. 213.

[32] Ibid. 209.

[33] Ibid.

[34] See John C. Meagher, *Clumsy Construction in Mark's Gospel* (Toronto: Mellon, 1979).

[35] Rhoads and Michie, *Mark as Story,* p. 1. Juel, *Messiah and Temple,* pp. 42–43. Robbins, *Jesus the Teacher,* pp. 9–10 et al.

Chapter 3

THE MARKAN PORTRAIT OF JESUS

... ———————————————————————————— *...*

Jesus, the Successful Leader

There are many instances in Mark's gospel where Jesus is accorded the acclaim due to a successful leader. He succeeds with significant numbers of people. Mark's gospel clearly depicts the marvelous works of Jesus and the importance of his message. This is clearly described by two modern scholars: "Like a Greek chorus explaining the meaning of events in a play, he will make sure that we, at least, realize that the story he unfolds is good news about the Son of God, in whom God's Spirit is at work."[1] "Rather, those traditions were used to announce that this same Jesus would very soon return, this Jesus who now lived with God."[2]

Proclamations

A series of statements which are identifiable as proclamations present a distinct picture of a remarkable personage:

1:1	The beginning of the gospel of Jesus Christ, the Son of God.
1:11	Thou art my beloved Son, with thee I am well pleased.
3:11	You are the Son of God.
5:7	What have you to do with me, Jesus, Son of the Most High God?
8:29	You are the Christ.
9:7	This is my beloved Son; listen to him.

14:61–62   Are you the Christ, the Son of the Blessed?
           And Jesus said, 'I am.'
15:39   Truly this man was the Son of God.

Thus, Jesus is clearly and systematically proclaimed both the Christ, the anointed one, and Son of God.

The proclamations are followed, explained and strengthened by those parts of the narrative which describe such happenings as: Jesus summoning followers; Jesus teaching and acting with authority and in consciousness of his mission; Jesus silencing and driving out unclean spirits; Jesus healing; Jesus controlling natural forces and feeding multitudes; Jesus attracting large crowds. Affirmations of who Jesus is and descriptions of his success with people are found throughout the narrative.

Chapter 1 provides typical examples of these actions. Without question, the opening verses are affirmative and proclamatory and conclude with a kingdom proclamation framed in the language of the early church (1:14–15). Jesus is proclaimed Son of God twice (1:1 and 1:11) and Messiah once (1:1). R.H. Lightfoot's analysis of this section seems to summarize the point:

> In the first eight verses we have learned that in accordance with prophecy the second Elijah, John the Baptist, arose and prepared the way of the Lord; but we have not yet learned the identity of the greater Coming One foretold by John; only in the verses 9 to 13 do we learn that He is Jesus from Nazareth of Galilee, and that He, Jesus of Nazareth, is the unique or only Son of God. By means of the story of the Lord's baptism and of the divine testimony to Him associated with it, and finally by a brief reference to the temptation, it is made clear that He, Jesus of Nazareth, is also the unspotted mirror of the Father's glory. Satan will put forth all his energies against Him in His human nature; but He remains victorious.[3]

Morna Hooker adds that "Mark has allowed us to see Jesus from God's angle."[4] The passage is clear proclamation.

The call narrative of 1:16–20 is typical of four pericopae in which disciples are called or commissioned (see also 2:14, 3:13–19, and 6:7–13). It is direct and unembellished. Jesus' word is powerful: he calls and men follow. There are no explanations given; motivations are not explored; no proofs of authenticity are requested or offered. The focus is on Jesus who calls. Bultmann has written of this section: "This does not involve any psychological interest in those who are called: the chief actor is not those who are called, but the Master who calls the disciples."[5] Jesus' call is not ignored. The episode depicts a great deal about who Jesus is and the power of the authority with which he speaks.

After calling his first group of followers, Jesus "immediately" begins to teach and to act with authority. These activities are first described in 1:21–28. Verse 21 is loaded with information. Jesus goes into Capernaum on the sabbath and teaches in the synagogue. "He does not choose the desert as the scene of his ministry, like the Baptist, there to summon the people to him. Rather he comes to the people."[6] The hearers are astonished at his teaching, mostly because he teaches with real authority and not as their scribes teach (1:22). Here, and at verse 28, the hearers draw a contrast between Jesus' authority and that of their scribes who simply pass on what they have been taught:

> For Mark, the contrast between the teaching of the scribes and the teaching of Jesus points to the contrast between the old order of things and the new, between the traditions of men and the power of God. Remembering what we have read in the prologue, we realize that the authority of Jesus is to be traced to the Spirit of God, whose power is working through him.[7]

There is no explanation of what Jesus teaches, only that he teaches with authority.

In verse 23 an unclean spirit makes the first of thirteen appearances of unclean spirits in Mark. This one attempts to engage Jesus in dialogue but he receives no response:

> The evil spirit makes the kind of identification which no human being, with one exception, will make in Mark's gospel story.... The evil spirit, recognizing Jesus and his authority, implores him not to overturn the demonic realm of power, but Jesus rebukes him, and the result is the convulsion and crushing defeat of the evil spirit.[8]

The unclean spirit proclaims Jesus "Holy One of God" (1:24). The same expression occurs in the parallel passage in Luke 4:34. Hahn proposes that the designation is equivalent to the naming of a charismatic person.[9] He denies the association of this title with Jesus as Messiah. Messianic or otherwise, it is a proclamation of some import.

Not only does the unclean spirit ironically know more about Jesus than the synagogue-goers do, but he is able to articulate in human language the identity of Jesus of Nazareth, who is known to his neighbors in Capernaum as the son of the carpenter. So the contrast is made between the well-intentioned synagogue-goers who recognize Jesus' ability to teach with authority but nothing more, and the unclean spirit who recognizes powers that go far beyond those of teacher. No explanation is offered as to the source of the spirit's knowledge. One dramatic irony has begun.

It is not made clear if the audience is able to hear the proclamation made by the spirit. There is no indication that the words are spoken privately to Jesus, but if they were heard by all, it is difficult to understand why Jesus commands the spirit to be silent in 1:25. The only hint of a solution to this puzzle is the description of the observers' amazement at his "new teaching." They know that the unclean spirit has obeyed him. In response they chorus, "What is this? A new teaching! With authority he commands even the unclean spirits and they obey him" (1:27). The response bears a strong resemblance to a Greek choral response.[10] The use of the device provides another way in which Jesus can be affirmed in a formula. It is a true dramatic irony that the audience's concentration on Jesus' teaching and his power over the unclean spirit muffles the sound of the proclamation that he is more than that. Nineham writes: "They are led not to recognize anything more than a high degree of that spiritual power with which they were familiar in other divine or spirit-filled men."[11] But it is very clear that the unclean spirit recognizes and proclaims who Jesus is.

The narrator summarizes, in a somewhat hyperbolic manner, the results of this first exorcism. Jesus' fame spreads through Galilee and the same type of wide-eyed adulation is recorded as that which characterized the response to John the Baptist at 1:5. At this point, Jesus is seen to be a charismatic leader who has followers and who teaches with authority. The narrator, the "voice," the unclean spirit and the reader know much more than this. The second part of the question put to Jesus in verse 24, "Have you come to destroy us?" contains a type of insinuation which characterizes many of the rhetorical questions in this gospel. It implies, but does not state, that one purpose of Jesus' coming is to exert power over evil. Jesus does not respond verbally to the insinuation.

Miracles

Instances of Jesus speaking and acting with authority are repeated many times: 2:1–12; 10:1–31; 11:15–19 etc. Summaries are used for the same purpose. Similar episodes where Jesus drives out demons are found at 3:11; 5:1–13; 7:24–30; 9:14–29. Jesus' first recorded healing/exorcism typifies many later motifs in the narrative.

Verses 29 to 31 of Chapter 1 contain the short episode of the healing of Peter's mother-in-law. In typical fashion the first sentence is loaded with information. It depicts the time, "immediately," therefore, on the sabbath; the place, the house of Simon and Andrew; the persons, Simon, Andrew, James and John, and the sick woman. The stage is set for a special, private healing. Only the four who had been called at 1:16–20 seem to have witnessed this sabbath healing. The use of "immediately" (euthus) contributes to the severe economy of effect by simulating a fast pace.

Matthew places the incident in a totally different context, a collection of miracle stories. This alters the perspective somewhat. Luke's account has one significant difference from Mark's. In Luke's narrative (4:39), there is no work performed by Jesus. He rebukes the fever and it leaves her. In Mark's account Jesus takes the woman by the hand and raises her up, a typical manner of performing such a healing. Mark's account of the method involves work and, as it is clearly the sabbath, one might expect some kind of a response. It seems clear that the narrator was concerned to portray Jesus showing compassion to the exclusion of concern about healing on the sabbath.

This healing pericope follows the call narrative (1:16–20), the teaching narrative (1:21–22) and the exorcism narrative (1:23–27). It adds a picture of Jesus caring for his followers, performing a healing without having been specifically asked to do so. There are no details given about the manner of the healing. The focus is on Jesus who uses no magical techniques. There is no recorded follow-up except for the service rendered by the woman. This does not add up to a *divine-man* (theios anēr) portrayal, contrary to the view of Morton Smith.[12] The recounting of the cure of Peter's mother-in-law is so economical and so muted that it actually loses some of its impact as a narrative of the power of healing. It is almost possible to read it as a non-miracle.

In terms of the over-all rhetorical structure of Chapter 1, this episode-pericope fits a pattern of contrast. The first recorded healing comes at a time when Jesus' fame is spreading far and wide: "And at once his fame spread everywhere throughout all the surrounding region of Galilee" (1:28). But this first healing is a curiously muted affair. The reader knows that a fever has left the woman. The on-lookers know only that a woman who had been ill is now waiting on the men. The wide-eyed adulation that closed the preceding pericope is not found in the incident of the healing of Peter's mother-in-law. Nonetheless, Jesus, who has been seen as leader, teacher and vanquisher of demons, is now seen as compassionate friend.

After the healing of Peter's mother-in-law, verses 32 to 34 describe the finale to the first day of Jesus' recorded activities, as the Markan author has constructed it. Mark's summary of the first day, through its diction, economy of words, and simple statements, lacks the thaumaturgic orientation of the parallels in Matthew and Luke (Matthew 8 and Luke 4). As Loisy writes:

> Il va de soi que la donnée de Marc, par la différence qu'elle met entre le numbre des malades amenés et celui des malades guéris, accuse un certain sentiment de la réalité, qui fait place, chez les autres évangélistes, à la préoccupation d'exalter le puissance du thaumaturge.[13]

In the parallels, Matthew and Luke use the hyperbolic "all" to designate the number of the healed. In Matthew, Jesus heals all who are sick (8:16–17). Luke makes it even stronger: Jesus heals "every one of them" (4:40–41). Mark only has "many" who were healed. Matthew is concerned to place Jesus in the context of one who fulfills the Isaiah prophecy: "He took our infirmities and bore our diseases" (8:17). Matthew has interpreted the words "borne" and "carried" (Isaiah 53:4) from the Isaiah prophecy as "take away," which Jesus does by healing (53:4). Luke's attention is directed to the demons' proclamation of Jesus as Son of God and the Christ. Mark uses neither of these orientations. His concern is to record the fact that, although many were healed, Jesus would not allow unclean spirits to proclaim him.

Verse 34 demonstrates the same element of dramatic irony as that found in 1:24. Jesus has been proclaimed Christ and Son of God to the readers. He has manifested power over sickness and unclean spirits. He has proclaimed the nearness of the kingdom of God. But the on-lookers must not know who he is. The demons may not speak of who he is for the strange reason that "they knew him" (1:34).

Some of the ironic contrast in this episode comes from the distinction that is made between what Jesus does and what is said of him. What he does is clearly visible and is responded to by those present, in the same way they would respond to any miracle worker. His fame spreads far and wide. Who he is will not be revealed to these same people, at least not by demons. The reader already knows. The pericope ends abruptly. It is impossible to know if the command is obeyed. The obvious laudatory nature of this summary typifies the use of summary statements in Mark to portray the successful teacher-healer.

While the first chapter of Mark records some typical actions of Jesus, there and throughout the narrative, miraculous incidents are used to portray Jesus as the charismatic Son of God. It is often possible to detect the tendencies of the *encomium* in these miracle stories, even when some indication of dissent or disapproval is included to create dramatic contrast: for example, the request of the townspeople that Jesus depart from the region of the Gerasenes (5:17). Bultmann has summed up the laudatory nature of the miracle stories:

> It is of the very essence of the gospel to contain miracle stories. The meaning and form of the miracle stories in the synoptics bears this out entirely. They are not told just as remarkable occurrences, but as miracles of Jesus. This is partly why healings preponderate and nature miracles are relatively few. Yet their purpose is hardly biographical

THE MARKAN PORTRAIT OF JESUS 41

in the strict sense. The miraculous deeds are not proofs of his character but of his messianic authority, or his divine power.[14]

Miracles, then, affirm the authoritative role of Jesus.

There are eighteen miracles recorded in Mark.[15] Of these, five are exorcisms, six are healings, three are "openings," two are multiplications of food, and two are calmings of the sea. In three instances it is the individual concerned who begins spreading the word or following him:

1:45   the cured leper: "but he went out and began to talk freely about it, and *to spread* the news."

5:20   the cured demoniac: "and he went away and began to *proclaim* in the Decapolis how much Jesus had done for him."

10:52   the blind man: "and immediately he received his sight and *followed* him on the way."

The technical terms, "to proclaim" (kērussein) "the word" (ton logon), and "to follow" (ēkolouthein), make these responses into statements of the personal mission of those who had been healed. They go out to proclaim the word.

Twice Jesus calms the sea with little effort and twice the disciples witness the miracle. The two feeding stories contain miraculous elements, even though their primary concern is not with such, nor are any responses recorded. It is noteworthy that, after the healing of the paralytic and the opposition of the scribes, "they were all amazed and glorified God" (2:12):

> Any psychological interest in the sick man and his friends is as far removed as it is in the story of the woman with an issue of blood. The miracle working word, Jesus' command and its execution which demonstrates its effectiveness are typical characteristics as is the impression made on the on-lookers.[16]

Since scribes had played a major role in the incident, it would seem that they too joined in the general chorus of praise.

A very significant portion of Mark is devoted to the portrayal of miraculous actions. The limiting of these actions will be discussed in the next section. Here, it is sufficient to note that, unquestionably, an effort is made to stress those elements of Jesus' activity which caused men to follow him, to listen to his preaching and to wonder who he was.

Teachings

Another significant portion of this narrative is devoted to Jesus' teaching. He is immediately recognized as one who teaches with authority (1:22). Many come to question him, having first recognized the alleged authoritative nature of his teachings. These include the crowd, the disciples, the Pharisees, the Sadducees. Jesus is called rabbi four times: twice by Peter (9:5; 11:21), once by Bartimaeus (10:51), and once by Judas (14:45). This indicates a reputation demanding a title of respect. The teaching passages indicate Jesus' personal appeal, his authority, his ability to withstand opposition, and his extensive knowledge of the meaning of the gospel he proclaims. They add much to his stature.

The author of Mark places predictions of the passion in three episodes after Peter's confession at Caesarea Philippi (8:31–33; 9:31; 10:31–34). These predictions must be seen, in spite of their content of suffering, rejection and death, as a very strong affirmation, repeated thrice for emphasis, that Jesus possessed powers beyond the ordinary. Lane stresses the importance of the predictions:

> The fact that Jesus' solemn declaration is repeated three times within a section entirely devoted to the mystery of the sufferings of the Messiah and his people indicates its crucial importance for the theology of Mark.[17]

In passages which demonstrably are very important, Jesus is pictured as having power to predict the future.

Joseph Klausner wrote of these passages: "If, after the crucifixion, the disciples believed in a suffering Messiah, then Jesus must, while still alive, have spoken of such sufferings."[18] In the same context, Klausner, whose interest is in possible historicity, refers to the passion prediction as a "supernatural vision."[19] In spite of all the problems the passage presents to the scholar, it is clear that Jesus is portrayed as having powers which far exceed those of other men. He possesses sure knowledge of future occurrences, including the fact that he will "after three days rise again" (8:31).

The same kind of supernatural knowledge is attributed to Jesus in the "little apocalypse" of Chapter 13. He is shown to be able to foretell the most detailed events in the future of his followers. Historicity is not the relevant question here.[20] The Markan author has made a claim about Jesus by his presentation in Chapter 13. He has portrayed Jesus as preparing his four chosen disciples for suffering and persecution. In doing so, he has added much to the stature of his main character.

Other Laudatory Elements

There are still other laudatory passages in this gospel. In all of Chapters 11 and 12, Jesus is portrayed as acting decisively, with authority, and with acknowledgement of his appeal from those who hear him. There is a distinct level at which they see and hear and accept Jesus. In the three main sections of Chapter 11, Jesus is portrayed successively as a very important pilgrim, as a cleanser of the temple and as curser of the barren fig tree. As Ben F. Meyer has written of these episodes: "The entry into Jerusalem and the cleansing of the temple constituted a messianic demonstration, a messianic critique, a messianic fulfillment event, and a sign of the messianic restoration of Israel."[21] In the final incident of the chapter, Jesus turns the device of the rhetorical question back on the Jewish authorities by refusing to reveal the source of his

authority. In Chapter 12 he tells a parable of the wicked tenants which they recognize as being told against them. He also
destroys the arguments of the Pharisees and Sadducees. He
comes to agreement with one scribe just before he condemns
the scribes as a class (12:38–40). He is totally in command.

The Markan passion narrative also portrays Jesus in a
positive light. He protects the woman of Bethany and accepts
her service. He calmly presides at the paschal supper and
emerges peaceful and strong from the garden. He withstands
and maintains his composure during the questionings.

There are other specifically laudatory elements in Mark's
portrait of Jesus. Crowds, having heard of Jesus' deeds, assemble with great regularity. Jesus is totally in command of his
work and his life and he regularly withdraws from adulation
and pressure for miracles. His calls to disciples are followed
immediately and without question. He commissions the
twelve to go out and to preach and to expel demons. Something of his identity is recognized by Jairus, by the woman
with the issue of blood, by the father of the demoniac, by the
Syro-Phoenician woman and by Bartimaeus. Either through
their actions, or through Jesus' comments, it can be seen that
these persons come to Jesus in faith and that he has rewarded
their faith.

Even such a cursory account shows beyond doubt that the
Markan gospel does, indeed, portray Jesus as a figure worthy
of praise and honor. It is the proclamations which tie these
elements together. Those sections of the gospel which are laudatory support the picture of Jesus as Messiah and Son of God.
He is the suffering Messiah whom Peter cannot understand.
He is the Son of God who performs the works that Yahweh
performed in the Hebrew scriptures: healing, feeding in the
desert, calming the storms. He is the teacher in whom the
kingdom is at hand. He is the agent of God who calls men to
believe. As all of these things, he is the subject matter of a
complete affirmative portrait in Mark's gospel.

Jesus, the Failure

The very fact that the gospels are the writings of the early church helps to authenticate the affirmative and laudatory aspects found therein. The negative aspects are not afforded such easy recognition. The negative aspects of Mark's gospel have often been noted and occasionally explained. They have not been seen as constituting a complete level of meaning. In the compilation, *The Passion in Mark,* Werner Kelber begins to approach the possibility of a negative level of meaning. He writes:

> If one refrains from reducing the Jesus figure by organiz-
> ing seemingly contradictory features on two opposite
> sides, a character emerges who is fraught with ambiguity
> and steeped in paradox. Jesus announces the Kingdom but
> opts for the cross; he is King of the Jews but condemned
> by the Jewish establishment; he asks for followers but
> speaks in riddles; he is identified as Nazarene but rejected
> in Nazareth; he makes public pronouncements but also
> hides behind a screen of secrecy; he saves others but not
> himself; he promises to return but has not returned; he
> performs miracles but suffers a non-miraculous death; he
> is a successful exorciser but dies overcome by demonic
> forces; he is appointed by God in power but dies aban-
> doned by God in powerlessness; he dies but rises from
> death; his beginning is nebulous and his future status is
> indefinite, and at the moment of Messianic disclosure he
> still speaks enigmatically of himself in the third person
> (14:62; cf. 8:31; 9:31; 10:33–34). If there is one single fea-
> ture which characterizes the Markan Jesus it is contradic-
> tion or paradox. It might therefore be argued not that
> "Mark presents two conflicting views of Jesus but one
> complex paradoxical view" (Dewey).[22]

It is noteworthy that Kelber's insistence on treating the portrait of Jesus as a whole is exactly the method that accentuates

the negatives. Any dramatic tension requires conflict or contradiction. However, the Markan narrative employs contradiction, paradox, antithesis, even what Frank Kermode calls "thematic oppositions,"[23] with consistency and continuity. The contradictory and therefore non-laudatory features, of which Kelber lists only some, are a major factor of an "intense opposition"[24] which determines much of the structure of the narrative.

In writing about the trial scene in Mark (14:53–65), Donald Juel describes the stylistic features of the narrative. He writes:

> One such stylistic feature of Mark of great importance for interpreting the passion story is the double-level narrative. The suggestion has been made, by other students of the Gospel as well, that Mark is telling a story the real point of which can be found only at a deeper level, at a level of understanding accessible only to the reader and not to the characters in the story. It has further been suggested that the most important application of this double-level of the story in the account of the passion is Mark's use of irony. The events are described to bring out the irony of the events—irony not for a character in the story who knows what the other characters do not, but irony for the Christian reader who knows what none of the characters in the story knows.[25]

Juel, then, bases his development of the structure of the double-level of meaning completely on the creation of dramatic irony. The second level of meaning is more pervasive than is suggested simply by seeing it as a tool of dramatic irony, but his description provides an indication of the right direction. Any student of Mark's gospel must somehow explain the level of meaning involved in all the misunderstandings, the failures, the lack of laudatory descriptions, the mutings of unusual happenings. These are the negatives.

Wolfgang Iser has written of the role of negation in a narrative:

> This (questioning of social and historical norms) is frequently brought about by the varying degrees of negation with which the norms are set up in their fictional context—a negation which impels the reader to seek a positive counterbalance elsewhere than in the world immediately familiar to him. The challenge implicit in the negation is, of course, offered, first and foremost, to those whose familiar world is made up of the norms that have been negated. These, the readers of the novels, are then forced to take an active part in the composition of the novel's meaning, which revolves round a basic divergence from the familiar.[26]

It would seem that the author of Mark was, indeed, using negation to force the reader to seek the positive counter-balance. He does not require the reader to invent this level: it is found in the text. The reader is forced to decide whether the negative or the positive level is to be espoused, or if they can be reconciled and formed into one composite, or if they complement rather than contradict each other.

Negative elements found in Mark's gospel can be divided into five categories:

lack of laudatory details of Jesus' life
treatment of miracles
constant lack of understanding
contrast with John the Baptizer
minor details

In some passages the negative elements are clear and precise; in others they tend to neutralize or mute a laudatory feature.

Lack of Laudatory Details

Philip Shuler identified the type of *bios* literature which is suggested by close study of the gospels: the *encomium*. He writes: "for this body of literature also has as its subject a significant and accomplished person who is not portrayed primarily through historiographical methodology."[27] The *encomium,* he asserts, was one rhetorical model for the gospels. He further explains the variety of topics, or *topoi,* that were most commonly used to achieve the portrayal of a praiseworthy man. *Topoi* are details of birth and early life, reactions of friends, family, neighbors, bodily excellences, virtues and noble deeds, posthumous laurels and the verdict of succeeding ages.[28] The first two chapters of Matthew's gospel and of Luke's provide excellent examples of the laudatory use of *topoi.* The narrator of Mark's gospel makes no effort to glorify Jesus by birth narratives nor by the description of extraordinary youthful exploits.

The narrative begins "in media res" and with the glorification, not of Jesus, but of John (1:2–8). Jesus is glorified in his baptismal scene, but the verb "*he* saw" (eiden) limits the knowledge of the glorification to Jesus alone (1:9–11). The narrator supplies so few details of Jesus' temptations in the desert that it is not really clearly stated who comes off the victor (1:12–13).

There are no resurrection stories in Mark. This makes his ending radically different from that in Matthew, Luke and the fourth gospel. One suspects that the author of Mark had just as much access to them as did the authors of Matthew and Luke. He chose, nonetheless, to close his account with a pericope that cannot possibly be conceived of as adding to Jesus' stature.

The only incidents where Jesus is seen in relationship with his family and neighbors are also negative in impact (3:20–21; 3:31–35; 6:1–6). At no point in Mark can the details of the early life, the family relationships or posthumous events be seen as laudatory. Laudatory *topoi* of the *encomium* type are totally lacking in Mark.

Treatment of Miracles

Mark's treatment of miracles reveals a practice of negating laudatory incidents. Only four of seventeen recorded miracles[29] evoke any response beyond the somewhat stereotyped and emotional one of amazement, astonishment and wonder. That these responses are, indeed, stereotyped and somewhat mechanical can be seen most easily by comparing them to the recorded responses in Matthew and Luke. Mark uses the words ekplēssō, ekthambe, ekthambeomai, and existēmai (in various forms) eighteen times. Matthew uses them five times; Luke, seven times. The meaning in Mark is almost always "amazed" or "astonished," admittedly strong words but made much weaker by consistent use. Matthew uses expressions such as "showed him reverence" (proskunēsan) (14:33) and "they glorified the God of Israel" (edoxasan ton theon Israēl) (15:31) and descriptions of actions which follow upon Jesus' teachings or miracles (9:26; 20:34 et al.). Luke stresses Jesus' spreading reputation (4:37, 44; 5:15; 7:17; 8:39 et al.). Four times, a specific action or response occurs, and in all four instances it is the significant response of following or going out to proclaim the word (1:45; 5:20; 7:36; 10:52). An expression of opposition to Jesus is recorded only once, after the healing of the man with the withered hand (3:6), and in nine other miracle stories no recorded response appears. This lack of response to the miraculous work violates the form which Vincent Taylor sees as normal for miracle stories.

> Miracle-stories are those in which the main interest is the account of the miracle itself. Such stories normally have three-fold form in which the circumstances, the wonder itself, and the effect produced are successively described.[30]

Only occasionally does the author of Mark allow a miracle story to become an occasion for adulation and praise.

There is also a discernible muting of the effects of some of the miracles. The healing of Peter's mother-in-law, for example, clearly occurs on the sabbath. It involves work at least according to the standard of Mark 3:1–6, "he came and took her by the hand and lifted her up" (1:31). The incident is related so economically and unemotionally that no response of any kind is evoked, not even opposition to a possible violation of sabbath rest.

The feeding miracles, described in rich detail, evoke no recorded response. It is instructive to compare these to the intense reaction to the cure of the man with the withered hand: "The Pharisees went out, and immediately held counsel with the Herodians against him, how to destroy him" (3:6). It is striking that there is no response to the feeding miracles which involve large numbers of people (6:33–44 and 8:1–10), in contrast to the strong opposition which results from a relatively simple cure of a single man. After the feedings, Jesus and his disciples get into the boat and cross the lake.

The work which Yahweh accomplished through Elijah is recalled in the feeding miracles (1 Kings 17:8–16). The Elijah motif is also present in the description of John the Baptizer (1:6), the raising of Jairus' daughter (5:21–43), and the questions of the disciples descending from the mountain of the transfiguration (9:10–13). The story related in 1 Kings 17:8–16 of the jar of meal and cruse of oil which are used but never spent depicts Elijah acting directly on command from Yahweh. Even more directly, passages about feedings in the wilderness are recalled. "I have heard the murmurings of the people of Israel; say to them, 'At twilight you shall eat flesh, and in the morning you shall be filled with bread'" (Exodus 16:12b). The same theme occurs in Numbers 11:31, Nehemiah 9:15 and Psalm 78:24–25. There is a very close resemblance to the Markan story found in 2 Kings 4:42–44. There Yahweh works through the prophet Elisha and feeds one hundred men with twenty barley loaves and some fresh ears of grain. It seems apparent that the Markan author is depicting the miracles of Jesus in light of these passages from the Hebrew scriptures.

The two calmings of the sea and the walking on the water (4:35–41 and 6:45–52) are concerned with highly laudatory purposes. These great nature miracles also seem directed toward reminding devout Jews of the workings of Yahweh in the Old Testament. The work of Yahweh controlling the seas and subduing tempests is recalled.

There are many Old Testament references to the action of Yahweh in parting the sea so that the Israelites could pass through unharmed (Exodus 14:19; Psalm 77:16–20; Isaiah 51:10). There are even more direct references to Yahweh subduing raging tempests: "Thou dost rule the raging of the sea; when its waves rise, thou stillest them" (Psalm 89:9); "Mightier than the thunders of many waters, mightier than the waves of the sea, the Lord on High is Mighty" (Psalm 93:4); and in Psalm 69:1–2 and 14–15 and Psalm 104:6–7 the theme is the same. It seems impossible to believe that, with so much resonance of the Hebrew scriptures in the nature miracle passages, the words "It is I" (egō eimi) could have meant anything less than a reference to Jesus doing the works of Yahweh.

Morna Hooker mentions this identification as a possibility:

> Again, in the second story, when Jesus walks on the water and says, "It is I," it is possible that Mark intends us to link these words with the name of God—I am. Certainly he would expect us to understand Jesus' action in walking on the water as an example of divine authority, since it was God alone who "trampled the waves of the sea" (Job 9:8).[31]

When one adds this possibility to the many references to the Old Testament in the passages, it seems to take on more the nature of a probability, almost a certainty. Therefore, the lack of recorded responses to the nature miracles of the calmings and the feedings does more than constitute the omission of a laudatory detail. It heightens the device of negation by deliberately minimizing praiseworthy deeds.

Lack of Understanding

A primary motif of Mark's gospel is the failure to understand who Jesus is by his family, neighbors, disciples and the representatives of official Judaism. It is important to note here that the Markan author has a somewhat inaccurate understanding of who the Jewish officials were.[32] When the expression "Jewish officials" is used in this study, several factors must be understood.

a. This picture is part of the narrative world which the Markan author created.

b. These "officials" would, perhaps, be more accurately described as spokesmen or representatives of the various groups at the time of Jesus.

c. The picture herein presented is of over-all opposition which was present almost immediately and culminated in the crucifixion.

d. The general inadequacy of Mark's understanding of the workings of that society perhaps explains why "chief priests" appear only in Chapter 11 and the Pharisees who have been consistently antagonistic are absent from the final chapters.

With the Jewish officials, there is no progressive alienation. They have made their decision against Jesus from the beginning. Some of the scribes had arrived on the scene as early as 2:6. They decide then and there that Jesus blasphemes (2:7). By the end of the first five opposition pericopae, they have determined to destroy him. The opposition grows until the crucifixion scene, where the chief priests and scribes mock and deride him until he dies. There is no progression, no reconciliation and no recognition of who he is or what his message may mean. These officials have freely and deliberately hardened their hearts. Therefore, they have refused to understand.

The pericopae of 2:1 to 3:6 form a unit clearly intended to stress the lack of understanding on the part of the officials.[33] This lack of understanding is played against the acceptance by the crowd (3:7–10), the recognition by unclean spirits (3:11–12), and the selection of the twelve (3:13–19). Then these positive incidents are contrasted with the disbelief of "those who were close to him," presumably his family.[34] The final appearance of Jesus in his own country merely emphasized the disbelief and rejection by those who had most reason to accept him. At no point in Mark is Jesus reconciled with, or recognized by, his family and neighbors.

The disciples who function as something of a foil to the disbelieving family until 6:6 take up the role of the disbelievers at 6:7. Immediately after the rejection by Jesus' own, the twelve appear in the scene for their final commissioning. When they return from their first missionary journey, they witness miracles and fail to understand. They continue in their lack of understanding until the scene in the garden from which they flee and appear no more. Again, there is no point of reconciliation and no recognition.

Finally, there are women who appear as a distinct group only at the crucifixion scene, specifically at 15:40. They stand far off and look on. They are also present at the entombment (15:47). They come to the tomb to have the stone rolled back, to find Jesus' body and to anoint it for burial on the morning following the sabbath. They fail in all three tasks and finally even fail to deliver the message that Jesus has risen. Yet again, there is no resolution offered and no recorded recognition.

Contrast with John

The contrast between the responses to John the Baptizer and those to Jesus constitutes another counter-balance to a laudatory presentation. In the first chapter, there is a description of John as a highly successful preacher. His success culminates in the baptism of Jesus. It is only after John's arrest that Jesus comes to preach. There is no evidence here, or elsewhere in Mark, that John knew who Jesus was.

Later, in the intercalated pericopae of John's death (6:14–29), two added elements stress the stature of John rather than that of Jesus. When Herod hears of the fame accruing to Jesus, he is afraid. He does not fear Jesus as Jesus, but as John redivivus. Jesus' presence is not fear-inspiring, but John's is. After John's death his disciples come to bury his body. But Jesus' disciples are nowhere to be found when it is time for the burial of his body.

Finally, in Chapter 11:27–33, the Jewish officials challenge Jesus' authority. He responds with a dilemma which defeats them. The officials cannot answer that John's authority was, or was not, from heaven, "for all held that John was a real prophet" (11:32). There is, perhaps, a subtle implication that John's authority could authenticate Jesus' authority. However one views it, it is clear that John's role is precedent to that of Jesus, and very important to this writer.

Other Negative Elements

In addition to completely negative aspects of Mark's portrait of Jesus, there are localized or specific examples of wondrous works and teachings whose effects are neutralized or muted. The use of details in some of the miracle stories is one indication of the effort to restrain the glory accruing to deeds which can only be considered miraculous. For example, as has already been seen, "many" are healed in the evening healings of the first day in Mark's account. In the Matthean parallel, 12:15, "all" are healed, as they are in Luke 6:19. The raising of Jairus' daughter in Mark is far from as clearly a raising from the dead (5:35–43) as it is in Matthew 9:18–26 and Luke

8:49–56. The same type of economy can be observed in the cure of the man with the withered hand (3:1–3, 5), the call narratives (1:16–20; 2:14; 3:13–19), and the release from the evil spirit of the daughter of the Syro-Phoenician woman.

The entry into Jerusalem in Mark 11:1–10 can be read as the type of holiday greeting often given to important pilgrims coming to Jerusalem for the Passover celebration.[35] The messianic implications are not always clearly visible:

> The key to the interpretation of the narrative is the strange combination within it of Messianic and non-Messianic elements.... Their cry is *almost* messianic. In speaking of the Kingdom of their father, David, they imply that the Kingdom is near, but stop short of the use of the title "Son of David." Their words transcend what might be said of a famous Rabbi, but are not full-throated Messianic homage.[36]

Bultmann regards the entry narrative as messianic,[37] but most scholars point out the ambiguity in Mark's account, missing from Matthew's and Luke's, but similar to the strategy used to provide less than a clear picture of the raising of Jairus' daughter.[38] In the crucifixion chapter, Chapter 15, the emphasis of the story is not on the crucifixion itself, but on events which surrounded it.

Another manner of muting effects used by the Markan author is the limiting of witnesses to various events and teachings, thereby failing to stress them. Only Jesus heard and saw the Spirit descending at his baptism. Only the three disciples and the parents witness the raising of the daughter of Jairus. The opening of the eyes of the blind man (8:22–26) and the opening of the ears of the deaf man (7:31–37) both take place after Jesus has taken the sufferer apart from those around him. The transfiguration is witnessed only by the three chosen disciples and the eschatological discourse is heard only by the three and by Andrew. Thus, the narrator of Mark carefully contains and controls responses to Jesus' words and teachings in many instances. He presents wonders as wonders certainly, but he is also careful in limiting the prestige and praise which would normally accrue to them.

The parallel passages sometimes employ the same type of limiting (Matthew 3:16–17 and Luke 8:51) and sometimes do not (Matthew 9:25–26 and Luke 3:21–22). The opening of the eyes of the blind man of Bethsaida has no synoptic parallel and the similarly secluded opening of the ears of the deaf mute in the Decapolis has no exact parallel. In both of these incidents Mark limits the effect by removing the action from the presence of observers. In all the synoptics, witnesses to the transfiguration are limited to Peter, James and John but in Matthew all of the disciples hear the eschatological discourse (Matthew 24:3–14, 23–26). The same discourse in Luke (Luke 21:5–36) seems to have been given in "the hearing of all the people" (Luke 20:45). The practice of the limiting of witnesses is not unique to Mark but it is effective in Mark in combination with other muting devices.

The Markan portrait of Jesus contains two complete levels of meaning, one affirming the identity of Jesus as Christ and Son of God, one negating or muting the successful teachings and activities of Jesus. Readers have little or no trouble accepting the proclamations and the actions which support the proclamations. The function of the negatives is more complex. D.C. Muecke wrote:

> Simple ironies always function quite openly as correctives. One term of the ironic duality is seen, more or less immediately, as effectively contradicting, invalidating, exposing, or, at the very least, modifying the other. In the light of greater awareness, or of prior or subsequent knowledge (sometimes supplied by the ironist himself), an assumed or asserted fact is shown not to be true, an idea or belief to be unwarranted, or a confidence to be misplaced.[39]

In the Markan portrait of Jesus, the fact that Jesus died completely abandoned on the cross and that the women failed to report his rising to "his disciples and Peter" (16:7) stands as unrelieved failure. On this level there is no possibility presented that he had not failed except for the vague hope generated by the words of the young man at the tomb (16:6–7). All things which are shown to be not true, non-tenable, unwarranted, misplaced, not believed are to be found on the negative level of this narrative.

NOTES

[1] Morna D. Hooker, *The Message of Mark* (London: Epworth, 1983), p. 16.

[2] Paul J. Achtemeier, *Mark,* Proclamation Commentaries (Philadelphia: Fortress, 1975), p. 3.

[3] R.H. Lightfoot, *The Gospel Message of St. Mark* (London: Oxford University Press, 1950), p. 17.

[4] Hooker, *The Message of Mark,* p. 16.

[5] Bultmann, *The History of the Synoptic Tradition,* p. 28.

[6] Josef Schmid, *The Gospel According to Mark: The Regensburg New Testament* (New York: Alba House, 1968), p. 43.

[7] Hooker, *The Message of Mark,* p. 26.

[8] Werner Kelber, *The Kingdom in Mark* (Philadelphia: Fortress, 1974), pp. 20–21.

[9] Ferdinand Hahn, *The Titles of Jesus in Christology* (New York: World, 1963), p. 291 and p. 380.

[10] James M. Robinson, *The Problem of History in Mark* (London: SCM Press, 1957), p. 71.

[11] Dennis E. Nineham, *Saint Mark* (Baltimore: Penguin, 1963), p. 76.

[12] See Morton Smith, *Jesus, the Magician* (New York: Harper and Row, 1977).

[13] Alfred E. Loisy, *Les Evangiles Synoptiques*, 2 vols. (Paris: Ceffonds, 1907), p. 457.

[14] Bultmann, *The History of the Synoptic Tradition*, pp. 218–219.

[15] See below, Chapter 6.

[16] Bultmann, *The History of the Synoptic Tradition*, pp. 212–213.

[17] William L. Lane, *Commentary on the Gospel of Mark* (Grand Rapids: Eerdmans, 1974), p. 293.

[18] Joseph Klausner, *Jesus of Nazareth* (New York: Menorah, 1925), p. 300.

[19] Ibid. p. 303.

[20] The literature on the thirteenth chapter of Mark is extensive. William L. Lane provides a good summary of it and of the nature of the chapter. Lane, *Commentary on the Gospel of Mark,* pp. 444–450.

[21] Ben F. Meyer, *The Aims of Jesus* (London: SCM, 1979), p. 199.

[22] Werner H. Kelber, "From Passion Narrative to Gospel," in Werner H. Kelber, ed., *The Passion in Mark* (Philadelphia: Fortress, 1976), p. 179.

[23] Kermode, *The Genesis of Secrecy,* p. 141.

[24] Ibid.

[25] Juel, *Messiah and Temple,* pp. 55–56.

[26] Wolfgang Iser, *The Implied Reader* (Baltimore: The Johns Hopkins University Press, 1974), p. xii.

[27] Shuler, *A Genre for the Gospels,* p. 37.

[28] Ibid. pp. 53–54.

[29] For method of numbering the miracles see below, Chapter 6.

[30] Vincent Taylor, *The Gospel According to St. Mark* (New York: St. Martin's Press, 1966), p. 79.

[31] Hooker, *The Message of Mark,* p. 44.

[32] See note 38.

[33] See Joanna Dewey, *Markan Public Debate.*

[34]Family is probably the correct translation of (hoi par' autou) since "his mother and his brothers" are present at 3:27–31; see Max Zerwick, *An Analysis of the Greek New Testament* (Rome: Biblical Institute Press, 1981), p. 109.

[35]Nineham, *Saint Mark*, p. 291.

[36]Taylor, *The Gospel According to St. Mark*, p. 452.

[37]Bultmann, *The History of the Synoptic Tradition*, pp. 261–262 and p. 305.

[38]See Schmid, *The Gospel According to Mark*, p. 204. Lightfoot, *The Gospel Message of Mark*, p. 45. Lane, Commentary on *The Gospel According to Mark*, pp. 392–394.

[39]Muecke, *The Compass of Irony*, p. 23.

Chapter 4

CONTRAST AND CONFLICT

· · · ────────────────────────────────────── · · ·

Contrast with John the Baptizer

The nature of the relationship between Jesus and John the
Baptizer furnishes some of the strongest evidence of a negative
level in Mark's gospel. The importance of John is emphasized
by the placement of his story immediately after the initial
proclamation of who Jesus is. He becomes part of the narrative again in the long intercalation about his death and burial
and in the disciples' questions after the transfiguration (6:14–
29; 9–13). His reputation is used by Jesus to challenge the chief
priests, scribes and elders with a dilemma about the source of
authority (11:27–33). William Lane writes of Mark's presentation of John:

> The brevity of his presentation of John serves to project
> into sharp relief two features of the Baptist's ministry
> which were of special significance to him: (1) John's career
> was the result of divine appointment in fulfillment of
> prophecy; (2) John bore witness to the supreme dignity
> and power of the Messiah, whose coming was near.[1]

John was, in the fullest sense, precursor. He proclaimed the
nearness of, not the presence of, the Messiah.

The Beginning

Mark's gospel begins with thirteen verses concentrated
upon proclamation. The rest of the first chapter, verses 14–45,

describes actions which support the proclamation. However, there are indications, even within the proclamatory section, 1:1–13, that a particular type of duality is at work. There is proclamation; there is muting.

The section 1:1–13 is comprised of four pericopae, vss. 1–3, 4–8, 9–11 and 12–13. The entire section is an introduction and, since it also provides evidence of the rhetorical nature of the gospel, may properly be called a *Proem*.[2] These thirteen verses contrast John the Baptizer with Jesus in a manner which clearly proclaims the stature of Jesus but does not always portray him as the dominant figure. The essence of the section is a declaration of Jesus' nature but the portrayal lacks some possible laudatory details and it mutes the proclamation to a marked degree. The omissions and the muting introduce the second level on which Mark's gospel functions, the level on which Jesus is totally misunderstood.

Contrast begins immediately. Verse 1 consists of seven words, six of which are nouns and one of which is an article. Clearly, verse 1 is a title and a clear, precise, laudatory proclamation of who Jesus is. The word "beginning" (archē) announces that this characterization will be developed throughout the gospel.[3] It may also indicate that the gospel itself is a beginning and that some type of follow-up is expected.

Who, then, is Jesus? According to Mark 1:1, he is the subject matter of good news: he is the Christ; he is the Son of God.[4] There is no supporting evidence for this declaration: it is not proved; it is not explained. There is no transition provided between the totally unproved proclamation of verse 1 and the prophecy-fulfillment formula which begins verse 2. Verses 2 and 3 refer directly to the precursor, the one who prepares the way.[5] This demonstrates one important rhetorical device employed by the Markan narrator. He uses a confessional-type declaration to declare who Jesus is, and then immediately directs attention to someone or something else.[6]

Verses 2 and 3 assume that the reader has some familiarity with the Hebrew scriptures. In a manner significantly different from that of Matthew and Luke, the Markan author uses prophecy-fulfillment texts only in this one instance. The narrator attributes the quotation to Isaiah, failing to point out that he has conflated Exodus 23:20, "Behold I send my messenger to prepare the way before thy face" and Malachi 3:1, "Behold I send my messenger to prepare the way before me." Matthew 3:3 and Luke 3:4 both use the quotation from Isaiah without addition. It may be assumed that the Markan author knew his sources at least to some extent. Therefore, his failure to acknowledge the diversity of sources seems to indicate a desire for directness of the type found in several testimony texts.[7] For example, Vincent Taylor writes of verses 2 and 3: "Mark's version is manifestly a re-interpretation of the prophecy in a Messianic sense."[8]

The composite quotation in verses 2 and 3 delineates John's role as messenger and precursor. Its juxtaposition with verse 1 and its nature as proof alert the reader to the rhetorical nature of the gospel. The identity of the speaker is carefully eliminated from these opening verses. Economy and abruptness strengthen the dual focus as well as the proclamation.

The narrative pattern which appears here is an important element of the rhetoric of this gospel. Verses 1 to 3 are pure proclamation. Verse 1 identifies Jesus. Verses 2 and 3 support verse 1 by describing the one who prepared for Jesus. The opening section of any narrative provides a locale of emphasis. A strong declaration in an opening passage would normally be followed by additional evidence. However, in Mark, there are two unproven declarations, related to be sure, but separate. Hence, two leaders are to be described. This double direction illustrates the Markan technique of moving the attention of the reader away from a proclamation to a related but separate matter. The intent would seem to be to redirect the impact of the proclamation.

The remainder of the introductory section, verses 4–13, consists of three pericopae: 4–8, 9–11, 12–13. John the Baptizer is described in verses 4 to 8. Robinson points out an interesting omission, "he for whom John is the preparation is not named."[9] This descriptive passage demonstrates a tendency to direct attention away from Jesus after important declarations. Achtemeier specifies the content of the verses, "For Mark, the content of John's preaching is repentance, and the announcement that he is only the forerunner."[10] The sentence which constitutes verse 4 describes John by telling who he is, where he is, what he is doing and for what purpose he came. This is a succinct overload of factual material for one sentence. The next sentence, verse 5, shifts to a more relaxed, descriptive manner which focuses on the geography and the universal appeal of John (all the country of Judea, and all the people of Jerusalem).

The technique of overloading the introductory sentence in order to provide the background for comments, comparisons, and descriptions of a more interpretative nature is found frequently in Mark.[11] Verse 6 describes John as Elijah, thus preparing for the references to Elijah in the transfiguration narrative (9:9–13) and the incident in the crucifixion scene where the Aramaic-speaking bystanders inexplicably misunderstand Jesus' cry, "Eloi, Eloi lama sabacthani?" (15:34). This descriptive passage seems to support E.P. Sanders' contention that "it seems that virtually everything which the early church remembered about John had to do with repentance and forgiveness."[12]

Verses 7 and 8, proclaimed in John's voice, contrast Jesus with John in terms of worthiness and baptism. John's words clearly point to the future and hence indicate that he did not know who Jesus was. Since the reader has already been fully informed of Jesus' identity (1:1), this constitutes the first dramatic irony. It is an important irony since John, who had been sent to prepare the way, would seem very likely to recognize

Jesus. In his study of the aims of John, Ben F. Meyer concluded:

> The mission of the Baptist belonged to a scenario of ful-fillment. His role was to assemble by baptism the remnant of Israel destined for cleansing and acquittal and so, cli-mactically, for restoration.[13]

The Baptizer's role, as Mark conceived it, was not to recognize and proclaim Jesus but to prepare Israel for his advent.

The exact parallel structure of verse 8, especially the emphatic "I"–"he" (egō–autos) structure,[14] emphasizes the difference between John and Jesus. John does not indicate that the Messiah has come. He thinks of the Messiah as one who will come at some future date. "He John does not give the title 'Messiah' to the one who is to come and this is no accident."[15] John's understanding of the one to follow him is strangely limited.

There is a grammatical problem with the phrase "with the Holy Spirit" (en pneumati hagiō) since Mark normally includes the article as he does "the Spirit" (to pneuma) in 1:10 and 1:12; he uses "the Holy Spirit" (to pneuma to hagion) in 3:29, 12:36, and 13:11.[16] This suggests that here the Markan author has altered his usage in order to accentuate the parallel between the two leaders. Only Mark maintains this clear and precise parallel. Matthew expands the description: "I baptize you with water for repentance, but he who is coming after me is mightier than I, whose sandals I am not worthy to carry; he will baptize you with the Holy Spirit and with fire" (Matthew 3:11). Luke also loses some of the precision of the contrast in a longer description:

> John answered them all, "I baptize you with water; but he who is mightier than I is coming, the thong of whose san-dals I am not worthy to untie; he will baptize you with the Holy Spirit and with fire" (Luke 3:16).

Both also include the image of the winnowing fan and the threshing floor. Mark's precision serves to keep the contrast between the two leaders in sharp focus: "Thus John the Baptist's baptism was recognized as marking the threshold of the kingdom of God but not the full entry into it."[17]

The basic contrast between John and Jesus which began in verses 1 to 3 is summarized in an antithetic parallelism in verse 8. Verse 8 parallels the two baptizers but distinguishes between the baptism whose meaning is found in the manner of performance and one which will, in the future, come through the instrumentality of the Holy Spirit. There is no evidence that John saw the coming of the Messiah as an accomplished reality: it lay in the future. The passage presents John as precursor and Jesus as far greater than John. This contrast is further developed in the pericope of John's death, 6:14–29, and the comment in 11:32, "for all held that John was a real prophet."

Jesus' Baptism

The motif of the action of the Spirit relates the two remaining pericopae of this introductory section, 1:9–11 and 1:12–13. As Robinson points out:

One is struck by the fact that Mark opens *in media res.* He picks up the story of Jesus at a point in his adulthood, whereas he had at his disposal (cf. 6:3) information concerning Jesus' background which he does not use here.[18]

Verse 9 forms the transition from the story of John to that of Jesus by a variety of stylistic mechanisms. The introductory formula—(kai egeneto), plus a time clause, plus a finite verb[19]—helps to signal the transition to a new focus. The time, "in those days," must be the time when John was baptizing because that is the action of the second part of the verse.

The preceding account of John was timeless, so the immediate delineation of a time element in verse 9 is noteworthy. Verbal echoes of verses 4 and 5 are heard: 4–5 (egeneto; ebaptizonto; en tō Jordanē Potamō) and 9 (kai egeneto; ebaptisthe, eis ton Jordanēn hupo Iōannon). The substantive and static nature of verse 9 is clear from the use of five proper nouns and two fairly static idioms (kai egeneto and en ekeinais tais hēmerais). It echoes the content overload of verse 4, describing when, who, what, whence and for what purpose. The strong and much used verb, "he came" (ēlthen), is weakened somewhat by the use of the two idioms. The passive verb, "he was baptized," points attention to John who baptizes more than to the one who is baptized.

The role of verse 9 in this episode is to specify time and place, introduce Jesus into the story and define his relationship with John. The dramatic irony is immediately apparent. This is Jesus' first entrance onto the scene. This Jesus, who has been proclaimed Messiah and Son of God to the readers, is defined first in terms of geography and then as one who receives baptism from John. There is no indication that John knows him as anyone different from the others who were baptized. The structure of the sentence stresses the coming from Nazareth before and more forcefully than it does the baptism. And, if there are on-lookers who have been impressed by the baptism, that impression involves John at least as much as it does Jesus. The final words of verse 9 are "by John" and such an emphatic position fits the structure of the meaning. This assumes that John was already known and that Jesus was not. Jesus is in the anomalous situation of being given authenticity by John's actions toward him. John need only "appear." Jesus comes from a specific place. The direct reference to Jesus in the first part of the sentence is somewhat muted by his passivity in the second. Be that as it may, John disappears from sight at this point and the prominence that his presence evokes is at an end, at least temporarily. The precursor who has enjoyed full prominence yields to the main figure.

In a manner similar to that of verses 4 and 5, verse 10 relates to verse 9. Verse 10 is more dynamic partially because it opens with two time references. The verbs "coming up" and "descending" function as an *inclusio* dramatizing a contrast between the very earthy act of coming out of the water and the heavenly action of the spirit descending. The nature of this coming of the spirit has been extensively discussed. The Markan usage of "upon him" (eis auton) differs significantly from the "upon him" (ep' auton) in Matthew 3:16 and Luke 3:22.[20] Lohmeyer discusses the point:

> Der Geist kommt "zu ihm"; Mt. und Lk. erläutern das mehrdeutige eis auton durch ep' auton, Joh 1:33 malt es aus: und blieb auf ihm. Was dieses Kommen bedeutet, ist nicht gesagt. Aber man darf es nicht als "Begabung" mit dem Geist fassen. Denn er ist hier nicht Gabe, sondern Gestalt.[21]

Ambiguity persists in the phrase "like a dove" which is one of the few similes in Mark. Therefore it takes on importance in the understanding of this Spirit. Bultmann explains the dove as a fairly common image of divine power.[22] However, William Lane points out:

> Several points of view are surveyed by R. Bultmann, *The History of the Synoptic Tradition* (Oxford, 1963), pp. 248–250; T.A. Burkill, op. cit., pp. 17–19, but for none of them is there strong Jewish support. They believe that the dove symbolizes the divine power which takes possession of the messianic king, but primary support is drawn from Persian and Egyptian texts.[23]

In spite of these important questions, the direction of the verse is clear.

The sentence of verse 10 is structured like an arc with "he saw" (eiden) as the capstone, the motion leading up to "he saw" and then down from it. The central position of this verb gives prominence to the limiting of the witnesses which it here denotes and which is an important element in the gospel. As the episode builds to a climax in the voice which speaks, it is clearly indicated that it is Jesus, and only Jesus, who saw the heavens opened. The association of the phenomenon of opening the heavens as an indicator of divine revelation is supported in many writings, for example, "The Heavens shall be opened, and from the temple of glory, sanctification will come upon him, and a fatherly voice, as from Abraham to Isaac."[24] It is not clear (but entirely likely) that Jesus alone heard the voice. A clear and open proclamation of who Jesus is, however, is muted by the limiting of the witness to Jesus himself; the use of the singular verbs makes this abundantly clear. This ironic muting of the effects of the proclamation adds to the store of knowledge of the reader but severely limits that of the participants in the narrative, if such there were. As Bultmann has pointed out, the elements of a call narrative are absent from this description, neither is it "a special calling to preach repentance and salvation."[25] It is totally proclamation. There are no explanations offered; no effort is made to explain why Jesus alone hears the voice.

The Temptations

In the final pericope of this introductory section, it is recorded that the Spirit "drove" (ekballei) Jesus into the desert. Verse 12 is structured in the same manner as verses 4 and 9. It describes who (the Spirit), when (immediately), what (drove him out), where (into the wilderness). It provides the factual transition to a new incident. It also provides the context in which the verb "drove" (ekballei) can be used for the first of sixteen times in Mark. In the parallel verses, Matthew has "he was led" (anēchthe) and Luke has "he was conducted" (ēgeto). In Mark, the Spirit controls Jesus in some way which is only stated; it is not explained.

Verse 12 carries verbal echoes of the preceding verses in the words "the Spirit" (to pneuma) and "the wilderness" (tēn erēnen). The verb "drove" (ekballei) denotes the casting out of unclean spirits but it also contrasts sharply with the non-pejorative, almost bland verbs of verse 13, "he was in," "he was with," and "ministered to" (ēn, ēn, diēkonoun). A contrast is also apparent between the vigorous action of the Spirit in driving Jesus and the totally neutral and passive Jesus who is tempted, who is with the animals, who is ministered to by angels. The Spirit is very active but Jesus is totally passive.

The thirteen opening verses of Mark's gospel, then, function as an introduction in the fullest sense of the word. The first word of the passage is "beginning" and it begins with a firm proclamation in the narrator's voice. It proceeds through further proclamations by John and by the voice from heaven. It contrasts the work of the Baptizer with the appearance of Jesus. The section ends on a somewhat mythic note that locates Jesus' role as victor over the power of evil. As Nineham explains, "that this battle has been joined is another truth known to the reader but not to the actors in the Gospel drama."[26]

Other rhetorical elements are observable as well. There is the beginning of an over-all dramatic irony wherein the reader is in full possession of the knowledge of who Jesus is. Only Jesus and the narrator share this knowledge. In addition, there is a stylistic tendency on the part of the narrator to make strong declarations, or proclamations, and then to shift the focus or point of view, thereby muting the effect of the proclamation. The effect achieved through this device is the redirection of attention from Jesus to the second referent.

The sentence of verses 14 and 15 is long by Markan standards: it has thirty-four words. it is weighted with substantives: twenty nouns and articles. The sentence again demonstrates content overload, in common with verses 4, 9 and 12. It tells when (after John was arrested), who (Jesus), where (in Galilee) and what (preaching the gospel of God).

The initial clause, "Now after John was arrested," does more than specify the time. It foreshadows the language of passion predictions and betrayals as in 8:31, 9:31 and 10:33. The clause defines the complete break between the ministry of Jesus and that of John, especially as the reversal of roles is reflected in the active "Jesus came" and passive verbs "after John was arrested." This reversal seems to indicate that Jesus waited, or had to wait, until the arrest of John before he became active. This adds irony to the portrayal by accentuating the fact that Jesus only moves into action when John is reduced to passivity.

Later References

There are three other references to John in Mark's gospel. In the intercalated story at 6:14, the narrator recounts the beheading of John. The story presents many problems but is important because it is the only incident in Mark which is known from an account outside of the New Testament.[27] Herod mistakenly believes that Jesus is John redivivus. He does not fear Jesus; he fears John. John is only the precursor, yet he is the one about whom Herod is concerned. The contrast is augmented by the final words of the pericope, "and they laid it in the tomb" (6:29) which are echoed in 15:46, "and they laid him in the tomb." The contrast is striking. John's disciples come to bury him; Jesus' disciples are nowhere to be found when it is time to bury his body.

John's role as precursor is clearly defined in 9:11–13. In response to a question from the disciples who had just witnessed the transfiguration, Jesus declares that Elijah has already come. Again, at 11:32, Jesus knew, and the Jewish officials knew (and the Jewish officials knew that he knew), that people believed John to be a prophet. The word prophet is used of Jesus only three times in Mark. Jesus uses it of himself in explaining why his neighbors have rejected him (6:4) and the disciples quote "others" as having called Jesus a prophet (8:28). The third time the word is used of Jesus, it is in mockery at 14:65. So, while John is believed to be a prophet by a significant number of people, Jesus is mocked and rejected as such. Again, the contrast favors John.

Jesus' Proclamation

The final two verses of the first section of Mark's gospel, 1:14–15, finalize several of the motifs of the introductory materials. Verse 14a dramatizes the gap between the ministry of John and that of Jesus. At 14b, Jesus becomes the focal point and the subject of active verbs, "Jesus came into Galilee." He had in fact come from Galilee in verse 9, but here it is emphasized because, clearly, Galilee is the site of his ministry, as Maria Horstmann writes:

> Es ist für Markus jenes Land, von dem die Verkündigung der basileia tou theou ihren Ausgang nahm (1:14 ff.) und wo dessen Offenbarung in machtvollen Lehre und in Wanderzeichen sich zutrug.[28]

Somewhat decisively, Jesus has come into the land where his ministry will occur and he begins to preach the good news of God. Mark seems to distinguish the "gospel of Jesus Christ" of 1:1 from the "gospel of God" of 1:14. This point is elaborated by John Donahue:

> Jesus, then, does not simply stand before the mystery of God; he embodies it and can be called "the parable of God" who summons the hearers or readers of his gospel to open their ears and hearts to "the good news of God."[29]

Jesus spells out the meaning of "gospel of God" in two participial clauses: "the time has been fulfilled," and "the kingdom is at hand." Jesus is the good news that God is acting in history on behalf of his people. The intervention is already occurring. The verb "is at hand" indicates an event so near that it is already operative.[30] In the final clause of verse 15, the imperative "repent" recalls the "baptism of repentance" of John in 1:14. It also foreshadows the apostolic mission described in Chapter 6. The call to believe in the gospel is a call to see the kingdom impinging on Jesus' power over evil spirits, in his forgiveness of sins, in his gathering of sinners. The hearers are not directly called to have faith in Jesus' identity but they are openly "challenged to decision in respect of the kingdom."[31]

The parallel text in Matthew has a different emphasis. In Matthew it is John who first cries out, "Repent, for the kingdom of heaven is at hand" (3:2). Jesus uses these same words again in the fourth chapter of Matthew which parallels Mark's 1:15. Matthew is concerned to show the continuity between the precursor and Jesus and has John simply and directly call for repentance. Mark treats the matter quite differently. John has preached a baptism of repentance and Jesus preaches that the time has been fulfilled. Mark stresses the role of God and the time and necessity for belief. In other words, Mark is concerned with elements which stress other things than simple repentance.

Bultmann has written that, in 1:14–15, Mark has prefixed to the narrative a summary in the language of the early church.[32] This is fair enough, bearing in mind that this direct proclamation by Jesus challenges his hearers, not in terms of who Jesus is, but in terms of the kingdom of God. Jesus is proclaiming the kingdom prior to bringing it, but it is so near as to be already at hand. Although most scholars agree with Bultmann that these verses are a formulation by the early church, their place in this chapter is significant for their rhetorical structure. They are presented as a proclamation in Jesus' voice, but the proclamation is of the kingdom of God more than of the identity of Jesus. These two verses complete the proclamations of the opening section, solidify the contrast with John the Baptizer, and introduce the concept of the arrival of the time of the gospel of God.

Jesus' Conflict with Official Judaism

The conflict of Jesus with those who Mark believes are the officials of Judaism is so obvious that to labor it would appear redundant. The point is made regularly that the synoptic gospels share this motif even from the historical perspective. E.P. Sanders writes, "Jesus did come into fundamental conflict with Judaism."[33]

David Rhoads says succinctly, "Jesus is in conflict with the authorities,"[34] and Joseph Klausner sees it as just as obvious that "the leaders of the popular party in the nation could *on no account* accept Jesus' teaching."[35] However, the particular constructions the author of Mark uses to portray the conflict and the points upon which conflict rests shed light on this particular negation. Some very precise questions may be asked about this conflict as Mark portrays it. Why was there immediate and unprovoked hostility on the part of the scribes and Pharisees? Why are the Sadducees mentioned only once and that in a precisely correct challenge to Jesus about resurrection? What is the real point of the opposition between Jesus and these officials? Why are Jesus' answers to their questions never enough to convince them—in fact, never enough to cause them to listen carefully?

Five Conflict Stories

It has long been recognized that Mark 2:1–3:6 is a unit consisting of five conflict stories.[36] The only debate about them has centered around whether or not the unit came from a pre-Markan source or was original with Mark. The relationship of the series with the eating motif has also been well-docu-

mented.[37] So, very early in Mark's narrative, it is made clear
that Jesus is in conflict with those who Mark believes represent official Judaism, specifically with the scribes, the Pharisees
and the Herodians. Michael J. Cook has studied Mark's treatment of Jewish officialdom and has come to the conclusion
that

> of the five conspiratorial groups as presented by Mark
> three do not merit serious attention by the historian.
> "Chief priests, elders, Herodians" may be simply general
> constructs, not technical terms or precise descriptions of
> authority groups actually functioning in Jesus' day (or
> ever).[38]

Although the inclusion of "chief priests" in this list is debat-
able, Cook's point is important. By careful utilization of
source materials, he concludes that it is no longer necessary to
distinguish between scribes and Pharisees, although the terms
are not used synonymously. His study shows that some of the
scribes were strongly oriented toward Pharisaism while others
were associated with Sadducees.[39] For the purposes of this
study, therefore, it would seem safe to speak of opposition
from official Judaism. At the same time it must be recognized
that the author localizes opposition to Jesus in the role of the
scribes who are openly hostile to Jesus on some occasions and
that Pharisees have a very specific role in some sections of the
Markan account, for example, in 7:1–23. Mark's use of the
names of the groups seems to indicate that he did not have a
clear knowledge of the distinctions or else he did not think
them important. The problem of identifying the officials is
inevitably complicated by the role that the Pharisees had
begun to develop by the time of this gospel.

Rhetorically, this conflict demonstrates the fact that no
matter what Jesus did or said, there were many who would
not, or could not, believe. The earliest example is found in the
conflict stories which constitute Mark 2:1–3:6. Each story

contains a description of a conflict, a rhetorical question, and a pronouncement. The use of rhetorical questions helps to focus the conflict. The actions Jesus performs in these incidents are similar to those he performed in Chapter 1—that is, he teaches, he heals and he exorcises.

The intensifying of the conflict can be seen in the following verses:

2:6 Now some of the scribes were sitting there, questioning in their hearts,

2:16 And the scribes of the Pharisees, when they saw that he was eating with sinners and tax collectors, said to his disciples,

2:18 And people came to him and said,

2:24 And the Pharisees said to him,

3:5 And he looked around at them with anger, grieved at their hardness of heart.

The opposition grows from thoughts in the heart, to questions directed to the disciples, to questions directed to Jesus, to challenge from the Pharisees and finally to Jesus' challenge to them. Immediately they begin to plan to destroy him.

The official opposition is immediate and total. The groups who oppose Jesus are listed as the scribes, the scribes of the Pharisees, "they," and the Herodians. There had been no provocation on Jesus' part prior to 2:1 and there is no satisfactory explanation for it after that.

In the first incident, 2:1–12, the author uses a variety of devices to ensure that the narrative functions on two levels. The narrator is able to perceive the thoughts of Jesus and Jesus manifests the ability to discern the thoughts in the hearts of the scribes; "And immediately Jesus, perceiving in his spirit . . . " (2:8). In addition, the author introduces the theme of the house and those who are inside, as opposed to those who are outside. Jesus forgives the man's sins because he sees faith, not the faith of the paralyzed man but of the men who carry him. No explanation is given for the source of this faith. The accusation of blasphemy, "Why does this man speak thus?

It is blasphemy!" (2:7), carries a faint foreshadowing of the
trial before the Sanhedrin.

The conflict in this incident is first made known through
the omniscience of the narrator. He knows that the scribes
question in their hearts and he knows what their complaint is.
In his turn, Jesus perceives "in his spirit" (2:8) and the narrator
also knows that Jesus can perceive their thoughts. Jesus
responds to their unspoken question with a rhetorical question in the form of a dilemma: "Which is easier, to say to the
paralytic, 'Your sins are forgiven,' or to say, 'Rise, take up
your pallet and walk?'" (2:9). Who could say which is easier?
Jesus' action after this provides the answer that physical healing may be seen as a sign of forgiveness of sin.

Jesus' part in this incident ends with the self-character-
ization, "But that you may know that the Son of Man has
authority on earth to forgive sins" (2:10). It is noteworthy that
Jesus uses the title Son of Man, which, regardless of all
nuances scholars have observed in it, is clearly the only title
Jesus uses of himself in Mark. Here, the statement he makes
is that he has *received* the authority to forgive sins. That spiritual authority is confirmed by the healing. The audience
response would seem to include the scribes who had been
questioning silently. The choral response stresses what they
have seen. They are not expressing belief. They are not passing
judgment on what they have seen. They are simply exclaiming
at its uniqueness. The hostility depicted clearly in verses 7 and
8 seems to have receded by verse 12.

The second incident, 2:13–17, is composed of two pericopae. Levi is called (2:13–14) and he follows just as the earlier
four had done (2:15–17). In Chapter 1, the call story preceded
a statement of Jesus' authority. Here, the statement of authority preceded the call narrative. Gathering of disciples is associated with a manifestation of authority in both of these incidents. Darrell J. Doughty summarized the extremes of
understanding about Jesus' authority and his relationship to
the self-identification "Son of Man":

According to Norman Perrin, this section of Mark's Gospel was "carefully composed by Mark in order to exhibit the authority of Jesus. . . . It is to Mark that we owe the actual use of exousia in connection with the earthly Jesus. . . . Here we have to seek evidence of Mark's own theological motivation. . . . Mark intends both to stress the authority of Jesus and to claim that he exercised that authority as Son of Man." These statements, however, have not found wide support in subsequent investigations of this material. . . . Our contention, however, is that Perrin's intuition was essentially correct. The affirmations concerning the authority of the Son of Man in Mark 2:10 and 2:28 are Markan compositions and represent a significant concern in Mark's Christological agenda.[40]

In the pericope, 2:13–14, Jesus' authority is manifested by men's responses to him.

The conflict intensifies when Jesus sits at a table in the house of Levi along with tax collectors and sinners. His disciples do not seem to be disturbed by what appears to the scribes of the Pharisees as a serious breach of proper table fellowship. The scribes challenge Jesus' disciples. Either Jesus is told of their opposition or he has overheard them. He responds with a pronouncement and adds another self-identification: as one who has come to call sinners. The word used for sinners in verse 7 is strong. It "is not the equivalent of 'outsiders to the havurah,' but refers to the most notorious members of their ranks."[41] The question is intended to evoke the response that Jesus is defying both the law and custom.

Jesus announces (2:17) that he has chosen to eat with sinners and outcasts. In Mark's gospel many of those who are said to have acted in faith come from among those classified as outcasts, as sinners, as unclean. These include the Syro-Phoenician woman and the Roman centurion, the woman with the hemorrhage and the blind Bartimaeus. So another element is added to Jesus' self-identification. He has come to call the rejected, the outcasts of the society.

The pericope of verses 18 to 22 contains a similar pattern. The conflict is described immediately. The question is asked and Jesus responds with several pronouncements. Even though the fasting was not a matter of law, it is obvious that an admission of guilt is expected from Jesus. Jesus responds with his own rhetorical question. "Can the wedding guests fast while the bridegroom is with them?" He supplies the answer along with two parabolic sayings. The stress that Jesus places on newness might have been understood in the light of the previous controversy. This time, the opponents come directly to Jesus with their problem. Jesus is depicted as bringing something new, or at least, as Sanders writes, "The question about fasting makes basically the same point: some of the traditional practices of Judaism may be foregone by those who follow."[42]

Verses 23–28 contain another pericope in the same pattern. Facts are given. It is the sabbath and Jesus and his disciples are walking through the fields. The Pharisees, who seem to be walking there too, direct a challenge to Jesus. Their question is worded carefully by the author, "Look! why are they doing what is not lawful on the sabbath?" (2:24). Jesus responds with a highly ironic question, "Have you never read what David did?" (2:25). The great proponents of the law seem not to have understood how David had acted in regard to the law. Jesus seems to be in closer contact with the law than the Pharisees are. This pericope also ends with a pronouncement establishing that, in Mark's view, Jesus is Lord of the sabbath.

In the final incident of the unit, 3:1–6, the conflict reaches its inevitable climax. The officials cannot tolerate being bested in argument. Their reasons for opposing Jesus have been shown to be that he heals and forgives, teaches with authority, eats with outcasts, and brings a new way of serving God. He even proclaims himself Lord of the sabbath. In the final incident of the series, Jesus challenges his opponents and is angered by their *hardness of heart*. Neither parallel passage, Matthew 12:9–14 or Luke 6:6–11, includes the expression, "hardness of heart." "Heart" in Semitic thinking is the seat of the intellect:

> [It] is rather man's liberty, the centre in which are taken the fundamental decisions; in particular the choices between knowledge and ignorance, light and darkness, understanding and what the prophets call stupidity, foolishness.[43]

Hardness of heart is the quality that prevents men from hearing, seeing, perceiving and understanding.

Following the pattern, conflict erupts immediately. Jesus challenges the Pharisees with a dilemma, "Is it lawful on the sabbath to do good or to do harm, to save life or kill?" (3:4). They do not answer. They cannot answer because the question is posed as a dilemma. Their hardness of heart prevents them from achieving any sort of belief in the man whose actions they have seen and heard, perceived and even understood; else why do they plan to put him to death? Their hardness of heart supersedes their seeing, hearing, perceiving, even understanding.

The controversy stories of 2:1 to 3:6 accentuate the negative level of the portrayal of Jesus. With little or no provocation, the scribes and Pharisees have become strongly antagonistic. The author constructs a series of episodes of ascending hostility to make clear from the very outset that Jesus was in deadly conflict with those this author considers the officials of Judaism. These controversy stories employ a closely knit rhetorical pattern that reveals the over-all dramatic irony that this Jewish audience, having seen and heard Jesus, rejects him in spite of, even because of, his obvious good works. He identifies himself in several ways which they should have recognized but they will not or cannot believe him. The inevitable result is the plot to destroy him. The author has used rhetorical questions to dramatize the fact that they have an inadequate reason for that plot.

Conflict with the Scribes

Immediately after the rejection by Jesus' family, the scribes are depicted in an effort on the part of the narrator to bring the two conflicts into relationship. Scribes have come down from Jerusalem to accuse Jesus (3:22). Their accusation parallels the one just made by his family and ties together rejection by these two important groups, official Judaism and Jesus' family. The grammatical structure of verse 22 suggests that the quoting of the scribes has special importance. The beginning of the verse reads, "And the scribes, who came down from Jerusalem, said, "He is possessed by Beelzebub" (3:22). The subject and its modifying clauses have been placed at the beginning of the sentence. The word order is important. "The emphatic word comes at or near the beginning of the sentence."[44] There is a manifest desire to accentuate the scribes as speakers. The abruptness of the change from verse 21, since Jesus' family and the scribes are not in any logical way related, makes the intrusion of the verses about the scribes even more startling.

The episode which describes the scribes coming from Jerusalem is part of the motif of official Judaism's conflict with Jesus. In this instance, the scribes clearly "seem specifically Pharisaic in their orientation."[45] The author artfully weaves motifs (rejection, demons, divisions) into a variety of structures. This addition to earlier narratives of Jesus' conflict with officials dramatizes and strengthens the theme of rejection by Jesus' family, at the same time that it reminds the reader of the continuing opposition of the officials. It also fits the presentation by Mark of extreme hostility which the scribes manifest toward Jesus. The depth of this hostility can be felt in the accusation that he is possessed by Beelzebub. Beelzebub was most certainly an unclean spirit although the exact meaning of the term remains unclear. The scribes have accused Jesus of having an unclean spirit. His family has done the same thing, as the use of exēstē in verse 21 implies, since madness was considered a result of possession by an unclean spirit. These two accusations, juxtaposed in adjoining verses, place Jesus' family alongside his professional enemies in making what is basically the same charge.

A second and separate accusation is made in verse 22. It is contingent upon the first but distinct from it. It is explicit—"by the prince of demons, he casts out the demons" (3:22). As Mark has presented this material, it is clear that underlying the charge must have been public knowledge of Jesus' activity against unclean spirits. If the scribes have been drawn down from Jerusalem to accuse him of casting out demons, his practice of such must have been well known.[46] Jesus responds to this accusation with the irrefutable logic that it is impossible for someone to cast himself out. Jesus' short, blunt question, "How can Satan cast out Satan?" challenges this hostile group from Jerusalem. Matthew 12:26 and Luke 11:18 have the words in a conditional clause, "If Satan casts out Satan," which moderates the hostility of the officials noticeably. By contrast, the scribes in Mark are reduced to the state of illogicality in their desire to discredit Jesus.

Jesus' question contains only five words in Greek, "How can Satan cast out Satan?" The verb used is ekballei which Mark uses consistently when discussing demons.[47] Jesus goes on in three parallel verses to explicate the ridiculous nature of the charge. He speaks in parables, one of the methods used in Mark's gospel to differentiate those who are outside from those who are inside.[48]

The parallel statements in verses 24 to 26, stressing the illogical nature of the scribes' accusation, come to a climax in verse 27 with Jesus' comment about binding the strong man. The point is made three times that any being which fights itself will destroy itself. Satan is no exception to that rule. The final words of verse 26, alla telos echei, may best be translated, "but he is finished."[49] As part of the contrary-to-fact conditional construction, these words make it quite clear that if the scribe's accusation were correct, Satan would, indeed, be finished. What Jesus has done is to turn the accusation into an ironic statement. If the scribes are correct, Satan's power is at an end. The real conclusion is found in verse 27. Jesus is not casting out demons by the power of Satan. He has just proved that to be absurd. But the accusation and refutation lead to the conclusion that Jesus has bound the strong man. As they have admitted, "he casts out demons" (3:22). He has conquered Satan and he has conquered the scribes by turning their accusations against them.[50] But no indication is given that they understood this or changed their thinking because of their defeat.

The change from verse 27 to verses 28 to 30 is abrupt. The latter verses bring the refutation of the first charge, that Jesus had an unclean spirit. The form of verses 28 and 29 is that of a very formal pronouncement. C.F.D. Moule describes it: "And then comes the terrifying statement that such blind jealousy which, seeing obvious good, deliberately calls this work of God's Spirit, the work of Satan, is unforgivable."[51] The blasphemy toward the Holy Spirit consists in attributing the works of the Holy Spirit through Jesus to the power of Satan. This amounts to a blatant refusal to acknowledge who Jesus is in face of strong evidence of his identity. It is a summary analysis of the scribes' deliberate blindness. It constitutes the ultimate irreverence to the Holy Spirit. Jesus strongly rejects the scribes' rejection of him. He has failed to change their understanding even by exposing their blasphemy. This constitutes another irony, since blasphemy was their first charge against Jesus in 2:7.

Verse 30 is an *inclusio,* one of the "signs of opening and closure."[52] When read with verses 28 and 29, it refutes the first accusation, that Jesus is possessed by Beelzebub, just as the binding of the strong man has refuted the second, that he casts out demons by the prince of demons. Since the subject of verse 31 is Jesus' mother and brothers, it seems that verse 30 is also intended to refute the charge made by Jesus' family. The "they" of verse 30 is grammatically ambiguous; therefore it is impossible to exclude the possibility that it refers to his family as well as to the scribes. It is noteworthy that Bultmann, in his discussion of the manner in which apophthegms developed, writes: "The most peculiar case, though it still illustrates the same laws, is where Mark separates an apophthegm from its original situation and introduces it into another so as to make double use of one situation."[53] The dual narrative of rejection by Jesus' family and by the scribes illustrates in strong terms the extent of Jesus' failure to make himself understood or, conversely, the failure of his contemporaries to understand him.

It is important to respect a structure that places words such as exestē, Beezleboul, echei and hoti elegov pneuma akathartov echei in such close proximity. This alone makes the passage carry a serious negative judgment about Jesus by representatives of official Judaism as well as by his family. It even stresses the parallel stances of the two groups of antagonists. It supports the contrast that relative strangers come when called and are willing to be "with him" as disciples (3:13–19), while his family and the officials of his country totally reject him. They fail to understand who he is and what his mission is. Those who had most cause to know him, in other words, do not.

Conflict with the Pharisees

Direct confrontation between Jesus and the officials comes to the fore again in 7:1–13. The pattern is similar to that of the five conflict episodes. Jesus is challenged by the scribes and Pharisees in 2:1–28 and he turns the challenge against them in 3:1–6. In Chapter 7, Jesus is challenged by the scribes and Pharisees (7:1, 2, 5). He responds, turns the challenge against them and goes on the attack in verses 6 to 13. The controversy of Chapter 2 revolves around sabbath observance, table fellowship and fasting. In Chapter 7:1–13 the focus is on ritual defilement. In this case it is a prescription of oral law which Jesus controverts, the historically enigmatic use of the term korban or gift.[54]

Lane points out a second parallel in addition to that with the five conflict episodes, that is, to the structure of incidents occurring in the first half of the Galilean ministry (3:7–8:26).[55] The two halves of this section are structured in the same way. The parable section 4:1–32 forms a central bridge between a summary (3:7–12), a call narrative (3:13–19), and a rejection (3:20–21) which precede it, and a calming of the sea (4:34–41) and three miracles which follow it. Similarly, 7:1–23 forms a central bridge between rejection (6:1–6), a call narrative (6:7–13), a calming of the sea (6:45–52), and a summary (6:53–56) which precede it and three miracles which follow it. The section is carefully structured and verses 7:1–13 placed in a position of importance. Verses 14 to 22 summarize the stand Jesus takes in regard to purity regulations and continue the distinction between those who are outside and those who are inside. This time the distinction is complicated by the incomprehension of the disciples.

Two incidents follow this controversy section: the cure of the daughter of the Syro-Phoenician woman and the opening of the ears and mouth of the deaf man (7:24–30 and 31–37). They demonstrate dramatically Jesus turning away from his own people to the Gentiles. He has been rejected by those who speak for the Jewish people. The break is made total here.

The incident recorded in 7:1–13 is not located in a chronological or geographical sequence. The author has placed the incident here for his own purposes. Matthew uses it in a similar context but rearranges it (Matthew 15:1–20). Luke omits it. In Mark, Jesus returns to Galilee only once after this controversy. He makes efforts to conceal his presence at that time (9:30–50) and is concerned exclusively with teaching his disciples.

The first section (7:1–8) is "an artistically stylized con-struction."[56] The scribes seem to have come down from Jeru-salem to watch the disciples eat. Sheer artificiality suggests a literary construct. The scribes watch the disciples eat and crit-icize them for non-observance of a regulation which was probably never practiced by the disciples nor by most of the ordinary people of Palestine. It is evident from the context that the disciples and Jesus were totally without qualm about it. Thus, the whole incident is probably a pious tale based upon some historical occurrence and used to make a point about oral law.[57]

The issue, at first, is a ritual purity law. The reader begins to suspect an ironic tone almost immediately in the gathering of all these important people to observe an everyday meal. The impression is strengthened by the irony of the ending of verse 4 "and there are many other traditions which they (the Phar-isees, and all the Jews [7:13],) observe." These traditions have to do with washing pots and cups. The narrator's aside in verses 3 and 4 connotes his ironic attitude toward the "build-ing of fences" around the law.[58] It also broadens the scale of the argument to include other regulations. The issue is the fail-ure of Jesus and his disciples to observe purity laws—the nar-rator is in sympathy with the disciples.

The Pharisees and scribes challenge Jesus with a rhetori-cal question which heightens the dramatic irony. "Why do your disciples not live according to the tradition of the elders but eat with hands defiled?" (7:5) The tradition of the elders to which the question refers is, according to Trocmé, "one of casuistry."[59] The efforts of the disciples to follow Jesus are in keeping with the true tradition of the elders; the scrupulous washing of pots and cups is not. Their ministry is synonymous with that of Jesus and equally in the tradition of Israel's great men. The Pharisees mean, by the "elders," the teachers of Jew-ish law whose regulations had been handed down and inter-preted almost without end. They are asking Jesus to affirm the validity of such regulations. Jesus points out the sheer hypocrisy of their question. Those who live by the commandments of God are in the true "tradition of the elders" (7:5) rather than the "tradition of men" (7:8). The similarity to the Beelzebub accusation in 3:22–30, the explanation to the readers in 3 and 4, the irony of the accusation, all help to remove this encounter from the realm of simple Pharisaic debate. It is that, and much more.

The author has supplied an occasion for Jesus to make very clear his position in regard to oral law. Verse 6 begins with another example of irony. The appearance of devotion to God's law does not reflect the reality of the Pharisees' lives. Their lip service to their own laws provides the appearance. The reality is that their laws have become separated from God's laws. They derive satisfaction from their casuistry. Man's authority has superseded God's. The phrase "Well did Isaiah prophesy of you hypocrites" (7:6), applied directly to his challengers by Jesus, is significantly ironic. The fulfillment of one of the great prophet's sayings about hypocrisy is seen in the hypocrisy of their laws. The irony ends with the accusation that they have replaced God's law with man's traditions. This is the answer to the original question. Jesus' disciples do not live according to the hypocritical traditions of the scribes and Pharisees, but according to the will of God (3:55). As he did in 3:1–6, Jesus has turned the dilemma back on his challengers and they are unable to offer any rebuttal.

In the pericope of 7:9–13 Jesus moves to attack his attackers. He transfers the discussion to the subject of God's law, and he is very specific. The meaning of the example he chooses is clear, even if its historicity is not. Jesus chooses an inviolable precept of God's law, the necessity of honoring one's parents, and shows how the practice of "building fences" is used by the scribes and Pharisees to place their own desires above the law of God. The pericope is completely polemical. Jesus attacks his attackers; there is no response from the Pharisees. The ironic tone appears again in verse 13, "And many such things you do." Again, man's law has superseded God's. This, Jesus calls sheer hypocrisy.

Verse 9 repeats in a bitterly ironic manner the contrast Jesus made in verse 8 between God's law and man's replacement of it which placed the oath before duty to one's parents. As Schmid has pointed out, "there is no mistaking the undertone of sharp sarcasm."[60] Through their casuistry, a duty commanded by God could be set aside. Jesus' objection to this seems to be almost a matter of simple common sense. One cannot use man's laws to abrogate God's. He continues the contrast by opposing the Exodus quotations of verse 10 to the sayings of the scribes in verse 11. The ironic contrast concludes with the final opposition of "making void the word of God" in order to support their own traditions. Jesus has destroyed their accusation that his disciples do not live according to the tradition of the elders by showing that it is the Pharisees themselves who fail to do so. However, even here, the narrator leaves the reader without a definite sense of Jesus' having been victorious. No response on the part of the Pharisees is recorded.

Some of the hostility of the Jewish officials is portrayed through incidents where they test Jesus to attempt an authentication of his identity. Four times in Mark's gospel Jesus is tempted. The Greek verb peirazo is used each time.

1:12   he was in the wilderness forty days *tempted* by Satan

8:11   seeking from him a sign from heaven, to *test* him

10:2   and the Pharisees came up and in order to *test* him

12:15   Why do you put me to the *test?*

All but the first of these tests depicts official harassment aimed at discrediting Jesus. The fact that the verb used about the Pharisees' relationship to Jesus is the same as the verb used to describe Jesus' having been tempted by Satan gives an ironic aura of the diabolical to these incidents.

The words the Pharisees address to Jesus, seeking a sign, are a test (8:11). Bultmann writes of the fact that the setting and the characters do not go together: "The author has Jesus in another territory and must in consequence bring the Pharisees out to him so as to create the opportunity for the words to be spoken."[61] He sees this as "an active tendency to present the opponents of Jesus as scribes and Pharisees."[62] The Pharisees ask Jesus to perform some sensational act to prove his power and his identity. This short pericope is related to the theme of seeing and believing and to the biblical test for determining the validity of a prophet's claim (Deuteronomy 13:2–6; 18:18–22). But when Jesus is asked to perform some wondrous work in order that they may see and believe, he will not do so. As C.F.D. Moule explains: "The claims of God can be known only by committing oneself in loyalty to him, not by standing outside arrogantly saying, 'Produce your evidence.'"[63] Jesus' miracles are not performed in order to force belief. He refuses to perform miracles for their own sake, or to point to himself, or to compel belief.

The Pharisees believe they have trapped Jesus on the horns of a dilemma, as they had tried to do in Chapter 7:5. They seem to believe that Jesus is unable to perform the sign they demand and that his inability will have to show itself. On the other hand, if he were to perform such a sign, he would be subjecting himself to their kind of testimony. As always occurs in Jesus' dealings with Jewish officials, the encounter begins with a hostile exchange: "The Pharisees came and began to argue with him, seeking from him a sign from heaven, to test him" (8:11). Behind the request is the implication that his powers are demonic in nature. "No doubt by a 'sign from heaven' (v. 11) the Pharisees meant some apocalyptic portent more compelling than any healing or exorcism. . . ."[64]

Two very strong indicators make Jesus' reply take on solemnity and depth. He uses the amēn lego humin formula which indicates that a solemn pronouncement will follow, and ei dothēsatai which, translated literally, means "if . . . will be given." This is a semitism which by implication says, "May God do such and such to me if. . . . "[65] When these two elements are combined with the words of Jesus' sighing "deeply in his spirit," the importance given to the demand and the response is clear. Jesus' definitive answer begins, typically, with a question to match the original one: "Why does this generation seek a sign?" (8:12).

Jesus refuses to give them their type of sign. Lane points out that Jesus' rejection is important historically and theologically. Its historical importance is found in Jesus' refusal to be judged by their scribal interpretations. Theologically, it is important as demonstrating their lack of belief.[66] Rhetorically, it is important for the light it sheds on Jesus' unwillingness to allow the Pharisees to demand a demonstration of who he is, because they demand to be able to understand that only on their own terms. Morna Hooker sees the negative import of the episode:

> Yet in 8:11–13, immediately after the feeding of four thousand men, the Pharisees come to him and demand a sign! In view of all that Jesus has done, their request is absurd. They ask for proof, and demand credentials. But what Jesus is cannot be separated from the things that he does and proclaims.[67]

Once again, representatives of official Judaism reject Jesus because they have closed their hearts to anything other than what they themselves ordain. They expect Jesus to be measured and on their terms and at their demand. The feeding of four thousand doesn't satisfy them even though it seems to be their kind of proof. Jesus effectively rejects them by departing to the other side. The gap between himself and official Judaism widens.

In Chapter 10:2–9, the Pharisees come to test Jesus for the second time. On this occasion, they are in Judea. Even though the basic pattern of hostile question from the interrogators, counter-question by Jesus, and then definitive answer given by Jesus to the first question is used here too, the context of the entire section gives it a somewhat milder tone. The pericope is part of a teaching section 9:33–10:30. It approximates the content of a Haustafel.[68] The question asked is only made hostile by the narrator's words, "in order to test him." Nonetheless, there is also strong emotion in Jesus' words, "for your hardness of heart."

The question and the response are based on the belief that Jesus had taught something contrary to the Pharisees' understanding of Mosaic law. The prescription found in Deuteronomy 24:1 had allowed divorce under specific conditions. Jesus does not deny this provision of the Mosaic law but attributes it to concession to the hardness of men's hearts. Jesus is "not abrogating Mosaic law but interpreting it more stringently."[69]

The real question being asked is, "What are the legitimate grounds for divorce?"[70] Jesus answers by going as far back as Genesis 1:27 and 2:24. His position is that God's intention at creation overrides Mosaic law.[71] The device of returning to the early biblical narratives seems to raise the level of the argument to some higher realm: concern over God's law, the law which precedes Moses. Many elements of this pericope make it seem a rabbinic-type argument without the type of hostility found in the other exchanges between Jesus and the Pharisees. Nonetheless, it places Jesus in opposition to the Pharisees, and has him condemning their hardness of heart. The narrator adds to the sense of confrontation by characterizing it as a test or temptation. It sustains the sense of controversy in the midst of the long teaching section.

Total Opposition

A second series of conflict episodes is found in the section 11:27 to 12:40. In the Markan construct, a series begins immediately after the threefold series of events: Jesus' entry into Jerusalem, the cursing of the fig tree and the cleansing of the temple. Inasmuch as it is clearly the disciples alone who heard the cursing of the fig tree, "And his disciples heard it" (11:14), the reason for the challenge from the temple authorities (11:27–28) must have been the clamor at Jesus' entrance into the city and the cleansing of the temple. In a manner not untypical for Mark, the dispute is delayed. Immediately after the overturning of the tables, those present stop to listen to Jesus' preaching. After that, they go out and begin to seek a way to destroy him (11:17–18). The second part of the fig tree incident delays the conclusion of the temple cleansing story. It is not difficult to understand that the temple authorities would challenge Jesus on the question of authority after an action such as that in the temple.

The series of incidents described in Chapter 12 bears every indication of being a literary construct. E.P. Sanders has written:

> There is no particular reason, however, to think that the Parable of the Vineyard (Mark 12:1–12 and par.), the further disputes with the Pharisees and Sadducees (Mark 12:13–34), the question about David's son (Mark 12:35–40), the story of the widow's mite (Mk. 12:41–44) or the "little apocalypse" (Mk. 13 and 11) represent teaching and controversy which actually took place between the events narrated in Mark 11 and 14.[72]

David Daube has written at some length that this series of incidents is "modelled, we submit, on a particular section of the Haggadah."[73] Daube goes on to postulate a parallel between the four questions asked in Chapter 12 and the four questions of the Passover eve liturgy. Regardless of the ultimate cogency of his argument, the study indicates, as does much other evidence, that these controversy narratives constitute a literary structure not unlike that of 2:1–3:6. One function of this construct is to demonstrate that opposition flows from all the influential groups within Judaism, or at least what this author thought constituted all the influential groups within Judaism.

The scribes seem to be the chief opponents since they are found throughout the controversy sections and the series closes with Jesus' outright condemnation of them (12:35–40). In the early series of conflict episodes (2:1–3:6), their opposition is unprovoked. Here, it seems to flow from the incident in the temple. They challenge Jesus about his authority to perform these actions, not about the actions themselves. Jesus' direct challenge to the authority of the temple hierarchy provokes hostility. As always, the authorities are restricted by their fear of the crowd. They receive a second impetus to hostility in the parable of the tenants (12:1–12) which they see as told against them. Again, their fear of the crowd is the retarding element used to permit the continuance of the progressive controversy.

The incidents told in 12:13–34, whatever else they do, are clearly intended to include what Mark perceived to be the major groups of Jewish officialdom, Pharisees, Sadducees and scribes. In the course of the events all of the groups are vanquished in argument.[74] Only the one scribe whose question seemed sincere is not demolished by Jesus' words, but even there, "After that, no one dared to ask him any question" (12:34). When Jesus' authority is questioned by the temple hierarchy, the response that the narrator provides includes a parable, three pronouncements and an open rejection of the scribes.

The first incident links Jesus' authority to the baptism and prophetic teaching of John.[75] At the very least, John's authority and Jesus' derive from the same source. In a manner similar to that of the first incident of the first controversy series (2:1–12), this opening exchange includes a question it is impossible to answer. The authorities face a real dilemma and are forced to back down. It is significant that John's stature and the authorities' fear of the people are important aspects of the officials' inability to respond. The motif of the crowd protecting Jesus is stressed here. The motif of John as a figure of great stature ends.

The parable of the tenants (12:1–12) is taken as an allegory by the officials. The "hearers" must refer to the "chief priests and the scribes and the elders" (11:27). They believe Jesus is characterizing himself as the son of the vineyard master. The reference to the Hebrew scriptures, that is, to Isaiah 5:17 and to Psalm 118:22–23, makes the point very clear to Jesus' hearers. Divine judgment will fall on those who have such clear testimony before their eyes yet do not accept either the words of Jesus or the words of their own scriptures. Once again they are prevented from acting by their fear of the crowd.

The three pronouncement stories neatly involve Mark's concept of the Jewish power structure. There is "little editorial material. The total effect is to show the discomfiture of those who approach Jesus."[76] The Pharisees try to trap Jesus into a dilemma which he avoids by indicating that their obligation to their overlords falls within the established divine order. They are amazed at him. Again, the stereotypical emotional response substitutes for any meaningful action.

The question from the Sadducees accurately presents one of their chief positions, that there is no resurrection. The absurdity of the example they propose is intended to trick him into a nonsensical argument and thus to ridicule him. Instead it provides Jesus with the occasion to point out their hypocrisy and to refute their position. In the previous dialogue Jesus' pronouncement left no room for counter-argument. In this incident he rises above the ridiculous example and speaks authoritatively in two counter-questions. In both questions, he insinuates ironically, as he had in 7:8, that the great students of the scriptures fail to understand their own scriptures.[77] They also fail to recognize the God of their fathers. As Jesus uses the term, "God of the dead," it is a contradiction in terms. The Torah requires belief in the resurrection: "And these are they that have no share in the world to come: he that says that there is no resurrection of the dead prescribed in the Law."[78] The Mishnah is clear. And Jesus is clear that failure to believe in resurrection is quite wrong. On this theological plane the controversy ends. Jesus vanquishes—rather totally it seems—the Sadducees by recalling them to the tradition of their own scriptures and of their covenant with God. And they should have understood all of this rather easily since: "Die pericope bewegt sich durchaus in den Geleifen rabbinischen Denkens; rabbinish ist das bizzarre Beispiel der Gegner wie der Beweis Jesu."[79] They are neither seen nor heard of again in Mark. It may not have been clear to this author that "chief priests" could have been Sadducees. Jesus has destroyed the argument of the Sadducees, but he has not won them to his side.

The final controversy (12:35–40) serves to vanquish the scribes. Jesus confronts them "in the temple" (12:35). He raises a question of paramount interest. He asks what the scribes mean when they say that the Christ is the Son of David. The point of the question is the proper understanding of the words Son of David as used of the Messiah. Jesus' purpose seems to be to question the relationship as it is seen by scribes in his day:

> Whether the point of this story is to allow Jesus to claim to be the Christ even though he is not of the Davidic line (Matthew and Luke make it a point to include information that he is, but Mark contains no such traditions about Jesus' ancestry), or to dispute the appropriateness of Jewish messianic expectation (the anointed one cannot be Davidic), Mark can simply allow the title "Christ" to stand as a normal designation of the awaited deliverer.[80]

The implications are important: Jesus has challenged a simplistic identification of the Messiah with a political-nationalistic concept which the scribes evidently espoused. By pointing out that the Messiah is Lord, Jesus has monumentally enlarged the concept. Where the scribal teaching depicts the Messiah as of human descent from David, Jesus points out that he is Lord, that his dignity and power far transcend their simplistic argumentation. Interestingly, the crowd seems happy to have Jesus on their side or, perhaps, to see the scribes put down. The Sadducees have been silenced and now the scribes seem to have been taken out of contention also. Although their arguments have been destroyed, there is no indication that either group, as group, has moved any closer to Jesus.

Jesus concludes the condemnation of the scribes and the description of his public ministry by castigating scribal abuses. He has already condemned their teaching as simplistic, one-sided and ill-informed. Here, in 12:38–40, he condemns their actions as self-intoxicated and self-serving, in direct contrast with the widow who makes her offering in the next pericope. The charges Jesus makes, of hypocrisy, of enjoying privileges, of imposing on the means of the poor, sound as if they are being made against the Pharisees. As usual, Mark distinguishes little among official groups. The lives of these officials do not accord with their professions. No response is recorded and later events would seem to indicate that the scribes were not impressed or were impressed negatively at being contested.

Final Conflict

The final conflict, of course, occurs in the passion narrative. There, themes converge. The author uses intercalation to contrast the woman of Bethany, who acts with sincerity and humility (14:3–9), with those who act with treachery, the chief priests and scribes (14:2). The scene has been carefully prepared. At 3:6 the Pharisees and Herodians have plotted to destroy him, and the chief priests and scribes do the same at 11:18. At 12:12 the same verbs are used when his family seeks him (zetousin) (3:22) and (ezētoun) (12:12)—and when they come to seize (kratēsai) him (3:21 and 12:12). In 14:1 and 2, the

chief priests and scribes seek (ezētoun) how to seize (kratē-
santes) Jesus. It is made clear in 14:1 and 2, as in 12:12, that
the crowd is Jesus' best protection against treachery. It is also
clear that the author means to stress opposition from the officials of Judaism. The expression " 'the Jewish authorities' con-
veys well enough the sense intended both here and in verse
10."[81] Perhaps a new motif is introduced here. The woman in
the intercalated incident merits high praise for her act of devotion. The woman's action introduces the passion narrative
which ends with an account of the women who act with courage and devotion at the empty tomb.

The two incidents which open Chapter 14, the officials'
plot and the anointing at Bethany, one of timid opposition and
one of courageous devotion, initiate Jesus' final rejection. The
Markan account is sparse and unadorned. Judas agrees to
betray Jesus (paradoi), to deliver him up or hand him over.
There is no exact motivation given for Judas' betrayal. The
causes for the official objection to Jesus are equally unclear—
he has performed good works (2:1–3:6) and he has destroyed
their casuistic arguments (11:27–12:40). Only an obstinate
rejection of the truth of what they had seen and heard, the
result of hardness of heart, can explain official opposition. It
is significant that there is no mention of the action in the
temple.

Donald Juel has reached convincing conclusions about
the narrative of the trial before the Sanhedrin:

> According to 8:31, what is important about the Jewish
> trial is that Jesus is "rejected" by the religious leaders of
> the people. That rejection, viewed as the fulfillment of the
> scripture (Ps. 118:22), is of obvious importance to the
> author.
>
> The author seems more concerned to provide the
> reader with a more profound understanding of this
> "rejection."[82]

The trial stresses the opposition of the Jewish authorities in spite of the fact that it has no causal relationship with the trial before Pilate. Juel has very adequately pointed out the difficulties with this pericope: the failure of the "planted" witnesses to agree, the failure to stone Jesus for his blasphemy, the question raised by the charge of blasphemy.[83] What is germane to this study is the clear fact that the whole council wanted to put Jesus to death, but could find no charges which would allow them that action. Instead of accusations about violating the sabbath (3:1–6), claiming authority to forgive sins (2:1–12), disturbing the temple (11:15–19), condemning the officials in parables (12:1–12), they propose an accusation that is false: "We heard him say, 'I will destroy this temple . . . '" (14:58). They label Jesus' claim to be Messiah and Son of God blasphemy—which it was not. To claim to be king was not blasphemy. The expression "Son of the Blessed" presents a series of problems which are discussed by Donald Juel:

> First, the term "the Blessed One," as a circumlocution for the name of God, is almost completely unattested in Jewish literature. Second, the title "Son of the Blessed" (Son of God) in the verse seems to be synonymous with "the Christ." But the title "Son of God" is rarely used as a messianic designation in extant Jewish literature which has led several scholars to assert that the whole expression, "the Christ, the Son of the Blessed," is thoroughly unJewish, Christianized terminology.[84]

Juel concludes from study of usages in the passion narrative of "King of the Jews," and "the Christ, the King of Israel," that "Jesus, according to Mark, is asked by the high-priest if he is the Messiah-King promised in scripture."[85] The charge, then, is probably non-historical and part of an over-all literary construct of the early church. That Mark intends the two parts of the high priest's question to refer to messiahship is accepted as a probability by many important scholars.[86]

Among the many conclusions that can be derived from the Markan account of the Sanhedrin trial is that it is a literary construct intended to stress some important themes. Two of the important themes are that the Sanhedrin was antagonized to a point of irrationality by its need to destroy Jesus and the fact that they could come up with no valid reason to have him put to death. Their taunting of him as prophet is surely intended as a dramatic irony since, at the precise moment that it is occurring, Jesus' prophecy in regard to Peter is being fulfilled. The opposition of Jewish officialdom (at this point the author has identified them correctly) is reduced to irrationality and has sealed Jesus' fate. Their rejection of him is now complete.

The chief priests, scribes and elders appear in Chapter 15, accusing him of "many things" (15:3). They had obviously told Pilate he had claimed to be King of the Jews since that is Pilate's first question to him (15:2). The role of chief priests is clear to Pilate and he attributes to them their real motivation: envy (15:10). The chief priests work the crowd into a frenzied mob, so that rationality can be in no danger of offsetting mob hysteria. Finally, the supreme dramatic irony occurs—the chief priests, joined by the scribes, mock him as King. The author is strong in his portrayal of the officials as blinded by envy, irrational in their own behavior, manipulating the crowd. He crowns the story of their rejection of Jesus by the tremendous irony that they very correctly proclaim him to be the Christ, the King of Israel. The readers know him to be just that. The author adds the irony that they taunt him to come down from the cross that they may see and believe. They have been seeing and hearing since Jesus first came from Nazareth, but they still have not believed.

The failure of Jesus to make believers of the Jewish officials cannot be laid to any specific action or actions of Jesus. They oppose him at the beginning of his work for no reason and they bring about his death for no clear reason except envy. This author takes some pains to point out the hardness of heart, especially that of hearts hardened by envy, that prevents any real belief by the officials. His depiction of the Sanhedrin trial, of the hearing before Pilate and of the crucifixion, all make it clear that no charges against Jesus can be made to hold. Simply and clearly, Jesus had failed to change the hearts of the leaders of the religious establishment and no valid reason is offered to explain this failure.

It should be noted that first century Christians would have found it impossible to accept any other result than rejection by the Jewish officials. They considered the whole history recounted in the Hebrew scriptures as a story of rebellion and hardness of heart on the part of the Jews. Nonetheless, this rejection by official Judaism should be recognized as the underpinning of all the negative forces at work in the narrative. The author of Mark used this common belief to support his use of negation. Expected or not, it is important to the development of a level of negation.

NOTES

[1] Lane, *Commentary on the Gospel of Mark*, p. 48.

[2] Marius Reiser, *Syntax und Stil des Markusevangeliums* (Tübingen: Mohr, 1984), p. 92. Kennedy, *Interpretation*, pp. 23–24.

[3] Taylor, *The Gospel according to St. Mark*, p. 152. The opposing viewpoint, that is that the gospel is constructed in the direction of this verse ("passion narrative with an extended introduction"), is developed by Marxsen, *Mark the Evangelist*, p. 132. Marxsen's position is untenable in this holistic reading.

[4] It will be assumed that the words are part of verse 1. This is in keeping with a considerable portion of the scholarship as in Metzger, *A Textual Commentary on the Greek New Testament*, p. 73.

[5] Werner H. Kelber, *Mark's Story of Jesus* (Philadelphia: Fortress, 1979), develops the importance of the "way" as a motif in Mark.

[6] Cf. 1:11 and 12; 8:29 and 30–31; 15:39 and 40 et al.

[7] See discussion of this text in C.F.D. Moule, *The Birth of the New Testament*, pp. 80–84.

[8] Taylor, *The Gospel according to St. Mark*, p. 153.

[9] Robinson, *The Problem of History in Mark*, p. 25.

[10] Achtemeier, *Mark*, p. 52.

[11] Cf. 1:9; 1:21; 2:1; 7:24 et al.

[12] E.P. Sanders, *Jesus and Judaism* (London: SCM, 1985), p. 109.

[13] Meyer, *The Aims of Jesus*, p. 128.

[14] F. Blass and A. DeBrunner, *A Greek Grammar of the New Testament* (Chicago: University of Chicago Press, 1961), pp. 145–146, and also Zerwick, *A Grammatical Analysis of the Greek New Testament*, p. 101.

[15] Schmid, *The Gospel according to Mark*, p. 24.

[16] Taylor, *The Gospel according to St. Mark*, p. 157.

[17] C.F.D. Moule, *The Gospel according to Mark* (Cambridge: Cambridge University Press, 1965), p. 10.

[18] Robinson, *The Problem of History in Mark*, p. 21.

[19] According to Blass-DeBrunner, the construction is an example of "Hebraizing." Blass, *A Greek Grammar of the New Testament*, p. 277, #442 (5).

[20] Taylor, *The Gospel according to St. Mark*, p. 160.

[21] Ernst Lohmeyer, *Das Evangelium des Markus* (Göttingen: Vandenhoeck und Ruprecht, 1957), p. 23.

[22] Bultmann, *The History of the Synoptic Tradition*, pp. 249–250.

[23] Lane, *Commentary on the Gospel of Mark*, p. 56.

[24] *Testament of Levi*, 18:6, in James H. Charlesworth, *The Old Testament Pseudepigrapha* (New York: Doubleday, 1983), p. 795.

[25] Bultmann, *The History of the Synoptic Tradition*, p. 247.

[26] Nineham, *Saint Mark,* p. 64.

[27] Josephus, *Jewish Antiquities,* trans. L.H. Feldman (Cambridge: Harvard University Press, 1965), XVIII, pp. 116–119.

[28] Maria Horstmann, *Studien zur Markinischen Christologie* (Münster: Verlag, 1969), p. 132. See also Joachim Gnilka, *Das Evangelium nach Markus,* 1 Teilband MK 1–8:26 (Zürich: Benzinger Verlag, Auflage, 1978), p. 70.

[29] John Donahue, "The Neglected Factor in the Gospel of Mark," *JBL* 101 (December 1982): 593.

[30] Reginald H. Fuller, *The Mission and Achievement of Jesus* (London: SCM, 1967), p. 25.

[31] Nineham, *Saint Mark,* p. 68.

[32] Bultmann, *The History of the Synoptic Tradition,* p. 341.

[33] Sanders, *Jesus and Judaism,* p. 270.

[34] Rhoads, "Narrative Criticism and the Gospel of Mark," p. 415.

[35] Klausner, *Jesus of Nazareth,* p. 376.

[36] Dewey, *Markan Public Debate.* There is an excellent summary of the previous scholarship on pp. 41 to 55.

[37] Werner H. Kelber, *The Passion in Mark,* p. 27. J.A. Grassi, "The Eucharist in the Gospel of Mark," *AER* 168 (1974): 595–608 et al.

[38] Michael J. Cook, *Mark's Treatment of the Jewish Leaders* (Leiden: Brill, 1978), p. 81.

[39] Ibid. p. 91.

[40] Darrell J. Doughty, "The Authority of the Son of Man," *Zeitschrift fur die Neutestamentliche Wissenschaft* 74 (1983): 161–162.

[41] Stephen Westerholm, *Jesus and Scribal Authority* (Lund: CWK Gleerup, 1978), p. 70.

[42] E.P. Sanders, *Jesus and Judaism,* p. 207.

[43] Claude Tresmontant, *A Study of Hebrew Thought* (New York: Desclee, 1959), p. 119.

[44] C.F.D. Moule, *An Idiom Book of New Testament Greek* (Cambridge: Cambridge University Press, 1959), p. 166.

[45] Cook, *Mark's Treatment of the Jewish Leaders,* p. 91.

[46] Lane, *Commentary on the Gospel of Mark,* p. 141.

[47] The same usage occurs in 1:34; 1:39; 3:15; 6:13; 7:26; 9:38.

[48] See below, Chapter 6.

[49] Zerwick, *A Grammatical Analysis of the Greek New Testament,* p. 110.

[50] G. Kittel, *Theological Wordbook of the New Testament* (Grand Rapids: Eerdmans, 1964–1972), Vol. III: "ischuo" by W. Grundmann, p. 401.

[51] Moule, *The Gospel according to Mark,* p. 32.

[52] Kennedy, *New Testament Interpretation through Rhetorical Criticism,* p. 34.

[53] Bultmann, *The History of the Synoptic Tradition,* p. 61.

[54] Taylor has a detailed discussion of korban, "Detached Note on Korban," *The Gospel according to St. Mark,* p. 341.

[55] Lane, *Commentary on the Gospel of Mark,* p. 244.

[56] Bultmann, *The History of the Synoptic Tradition,* p. 18.

[57] Ibid. pp. 17–18.

[58] "Pirke Aboth," in Charles Taylor, *The Sayings of the Jewish Fathers* (New York: KTAV, 1969). I:1.

[59] Etienne Trocmé, *The Formation of the Gospel according to Mark* (Philadelphia: Westminster, 1975), p. 99.

[60] Schmid, *The Gospel according to Mark,* p. 137.

[61] Bultmann, *The History of the Synoptic Tradition,* p. 52.

[62] Ibid.

[63] C.F.D. Moule, *The Gospel according to Mark,* p. 61.

[64] Nineham, *Saint Mark,* p. 210.

[65] Zerwick, *A Grammatical Analysis of the Greek New Testament,* p. 131.

[66] Lane, *Commentary on the Gospel of Mark,* p. 278.

[67] Hooker, *The Message of Mark,* p. 60.

[68] Sherman E. Johnson, *The Gospel according to St. Mark* (London: Black, 1972), p. 169.

[69] Sanders, *Jesus and Judaism,* p. 256.

[70] Nineham, *Saint Mark,* p. 260.

[71] Westerholm, *Jesus and Scribal Authority,* p. 120.

[72] Sanders, *Jesus and Judaism,* p. 305.

[73] David Daube, "The Earliest Structure of the Gospels," *New Testament Studies* 5, (1958–59): 180.

[74] Additional examples are found in 11:33; 12:12; 12:17; 12:27; 12:35–40.

[75] Ernest Best, *The Temptation and the Passion: The Markan Soteriology* (Cambridge: Cambridge University Press, 1965), p. 86.

[76] Ibid. pp. 86–87.

[77] Johnson, *The Gospel according to St. Mark.,* p. 201. Schmid, *The Gospel according to Mark,* p. 224 et al.

[78] Sanhedrin 10:1. *The Messiah,* trans. Herbert Danby (Oxford: University Press, 1933), p. 397.

[79] Lohmeyer, *Das Evangelium des Markus,* p. 257.

[80] Achtemeier, *Mark,* p. 43.

[81] Nineham, *Saint Mark,* p. 374.

[82] Juel, *Messiah and Temple,* pp. 66–67.

[83] Ibid. p. 65.

[84] Ibid. p. 82.

[85] Ibid.

[86] For example, Nineham, *Saint Mark,* pp. 403–405. Hahn, *The Titles of Jesus in Christology,* p. 130. Perrin, "The High Priest's Question and Jesus' Answer," in Kelber, *The Passion in Mark,* pp. 80–89.

Chapter 5

FAILURES WITH HIS OWN

... ————————————————————————— ...

The Failure with the Disciples

The failure of Jesus to bring the disciples to faith or even
to understanding has been long noted and often discussed.[1]
Robert Tannehill has pointed out that the "disciples' story has
come to a disastrous conclusion and the author has spared
nothing in emphasizing the disaster."[2] Paul Achtemeier writes
that "if there is any progression in the picture Mark paints of
the disciples, it appears to be from bad to worse."[3]

The Twelve

It is germane to this discussion that the disciples, or "the
twelve," are used as a foil to the unbelief of Jesus' family and
friends from 3:13 to 6:13. Their appearances up to 6:13 are in
the context of call and commissioning narratives. Once the
family and friends have disappeared from the scene (6:6a), the
disciples take on the role of those who see, hear, perceive but
fail to understand or believe.

Beginning with the first feeding narrative (6:35–44), the
focus of misunderstanding shifts to the disciples. Those who
follow Jesus are identified as disciples forty-five times and as
"the twelve" ten times. The expression "the twelve" is identified with being sent, with being apostle in 3:13–19 and 6:7–
13. Four of the ten uses of "the twelve" occur in Chapter 14.
Three of the four times it is used to identify Judas as "one of
the twelve." The other use in that chapter is in verse 17, "And

when it was evening he came with the twelve" to the final supper. In verse 12 the disciples are mentioned and two of them are sent to prepare the supper. So some disciples, at least two other than "the twelve," were present, even if only to serve.

Previous to Chapter 14, the expression is used in two contexts. It is clearly at home in the call narratives of 3:14 and 6:7 and it is used when Jesus explains meanings of things which are not made clear to all of his hearers as in 4:10, 9:35 and 10:32. In each case, "the twelve" are separated out, but other disciples are also present:

4:10	those who were about him with the twelve
9:31–35	For he was teaching his disciples . . . and he sat down and called the twelve
10:32	and those who followed were afraid. And taking the twelve again . . .

Only once are "the twelve" mentioned by themselves. This occurs at 11:11: "he went out to Bethany with the twelve." However, when they return in the morning, his disciples hear him curse the fig tree, so they were present although not mentioned. It seems possible, then, to discern a tendency in Mark to speak of "the twelve" as a separate group within the group of disciples. It also seems to have been important to identify Judas as "one of the twelve" (3:19; 14:10; 14:20; 14:43). On some occasions, "the twelve" receive special explanation. With these more or less minor precisions, "the twelve" as a unit melt into the group consistently referred to as disciples. As Trocmé has pointed out, "in Mark, more than any of the other gospels, Jesus is everywhere in the company of his disciples."[4]

The Disciples Misunderstand

Verse 52 of Chapter 6 returns to the motif of misunderstanding which had disappeared after the failure with the family in 6:1–6. Jesus has just fed five thousand people (6:35–44), then he has walked on the sea and calmed the wind (6:49–51). The disciples are beside themselves (6:51) (existanto): the verb is the same as that used by his family to explain his strange behavior in 3:21. It means that they are utterly and completely overwhelmed by wonder and astonishment. The narrator has described the great fear the disciples experienced at seeing Jesus. That fact betrays their failure to understand anything about who he is. All that Jesus has done and has taught to this point seems to have been useless to the disciples. Jesus has asked them to open their hearts (6:50), and after two incidents which may be intended to mirror the works of Yahweh in the Old Testament, he employs an expression "It is I," of which Cranfield writes: "It is conceivable that Mark intends his readers to be reminded of the OT use of the expression in Exod. 3:14 etc."[5] The disciples' concentration seems to have been totally on miracles to the exclusion of any perception about the identity of the miracle worker. They do not see Jesus within the context of the Hebrew Scriptures nor as someone empowered by Yahweh.

Verse 52a reads, "for they did not understand about the loaves." Here, the narrator's voice intrudes to explain their ignorance. Somehow the disciples, who had distributed bread to five thousand people and had collected twelve baskets of leftovers, did not understand much of what had happened. Their problem could not be a matter of knowledge—they had seen, heard, touched. It must have been a matter of belief—they could not allow themselves to accept as real the evidence which was before them. The message is very clear. Jesus is working miracles, perhaps even doing what Yahweh did in the Hebrew scriptures. His disciples cannot or will not accept that. Achtemeier believes that they could not, "but, in one instance, at least, they had no possibility of understanding. Their hearts were hardened."[6]

The narrator, still in his own voice, offers the reason, "but their hearts were hardened" (6:52b). It has been suggested that by Mark's time the word "hardened" (pōrousthai) was "used almost technically in the New Testament to describe the blindness of Israel in not accepting the good news"[7] (cf. 3:5; 8:17; 10:5). This is probably accurate in spite of the fact that the word does not appear in the Septuagint. The concept of understanding is specifically linked with this word at 8:17: "Do you not yet perceive or understand? Are your hearts hardened?" Knowledge is one thing that they had without question. Understanding is something else. "Thus the problem of 'understanding' is removed from either an intellectual or a psychological context, and is endowed with the theological overtones which accompany the idea of 'hardness of heart' in the Old Testament history of God's people."[8] Either they had not been given understanding or they had not accepted it. It is not totally clear which of these is operative at 6:52 but by 8:17 it is very clear. They, the chosen followers, had not opened their hearts to the reality that was before them. The structure and the narrator's comments make the lack of understanding complete. It would be difficult to provide more impressive grounds for understanding than those described in 6:35–51, the feeding of five thousand people, Jesus walking on the water and calming the storm. But with all of this before their eyes, the disciples failed to understand. They have, indeed, replaced Jesus' family as the ones who should have understood and did not.

In the parallel account in Matthew 14:13–33, the events are quite similar. However, Jesus' coming to them walking on the sea is followed by the enigmatic episode of Peter's walking on the water (14:28–32). The result of these two episodes in Matthew is the direct opposite of the result of the single episode in Mark. In Matthew 14:33, "those in the boat worshiped him, saying, 'Truly you are the Son of God.'" Mark 6:52 records the opposite result, "They were utterly astounded, for they did not understand about the loaves, but their hearts were hardened." Mark's sentence stands out in stark relief. No wonders, no self-identification by Jesus can pierce the disciples' unwillingness or inability to follow; 6:52 provides clear indication that the focus of lack of understanding has shifted to the disciples. The impression is not lessened by verse 54, "when they got out of the boat, immediately *the people* recognized him."

In the long, for Mark, teaching section 7:1–23, another direct comment is made about the disciples' lack of understanding. They are mentioned specifically in verses 17–23. Since the Pharisees have questioned Jesus about his disciples in verses 2 and 5, and the disciples question Jesus about the teaching metaphor of verse 15, it can be assumed that disciples are among those present for all of this teaching section. Certainly they are part of the crowd who are called to hear and understand (14). As in 6:52, the verb used is sunete. In 6:52, lack of understanding is specifically joined to hardness of heart. In 7:18 it is not so joined.

In verse 17, Jesus is described as performing what becomes in Mark an almost ritual withdrawal from the crowd (cf. 4:10; 9:28; 10:10 et al.). The disciples, evidently in chorus, ask for an explanation of the non-literal language as they had asked for an explanation of the parable in 4:10. Jesus reveals in verse 18 how incomprehensible their lack of understanding really is—and the theme of total lack of understanding on the part of the others seems operative also, as the words "all of you" in verse 14 make clear. The subject matter here is the law of purity, a subject upon which Jesus and the Pharisees could hardly have agreed, given Mark's assumptions. The disciples obviously had few qualms about eating with unwashed hands (verse 2), so the request for an explanation must be due to the utterance in verse 15 which seemed obscure to them. There is a somewhat curious mixing of initiatives. Jesus called the people, entered the house and left the people, but the disciples seek the explanation. The house has been a place of revelation in 1:29–31; 2:1–12; 2:15–17 et al. Here it is the place where disciples request a revelation:

> The parable of what defiles calls for understanding (14, 18) but the interpretation consists less in adding any new insight to the discussion of verses 1–14 than in pressing home a conclusion (cleansing of all food) which was difficult for some to accept.[9]

The lack of understanding is here specifically related to purity laws and practices.

Jesus' question in verse 18—"Then are you also without understanding . . . ?"—seems to indicate genuine surprise as well as disappointment. He seems to be saying that, inasmuch as they did indeed eat without ritual purification, they should have understood that they were putting into practice his dictum that what is external to a man does not defile him. When he questions their lack of understanding, he reveals that they have acted out a correct attitude toward ritual without realizing that that is what they are doing. The irony is obvious. Schweizer points out, "He [Mark] is not concerned simply to present a rational explanation because all this merely seems to reveal the incomprehensible blindness of the disciples."[10]

Verse 19, still in Jesus' voice, stresses the role of the heart as center of the personality.[11] It is essential that the heart be open, not just to the facts of what Jesus does, but to the understanding of his actions, to total acceptance of the full meaning of what he does. As in so many other instances, the disciples know and do, but do not seek understanding.

There is an interesting parallel in Matthew 15:1–20. Mark writes, "Hear me, all of you, and understand" (7:14). Matthew writes, "Hear and understand" (15:10). Mark, then, assumes a relationship to the crowd that is not present in the Matthean text. "Hear me" is more personal and assumes a relationship. This, of course, dramatizes the distinction between the crowd to whom the teaching is proffered and the disciples who are expected to understand it: "Then are you also without understanding? Do you not see . . . ?" (7:18). In Matthew's account it is Peter who asks for the explanation of the saying. Mark has the disciples ask in the somewhat artificial form of the chorus because it is now, clearly, the disciples who are cast in the role of lacking understanding. Matthew is not as concerned to make a point about the disciples as Mark is.

The Markan author uses the structure of the chapter to complete the contrast. Jesus is in direct controversy with the Pharisees (7:1–23) and his own disciples fail to understand. His family and neighbors have already rejected Jesus; the failure of those who might reasonably be expected to understand is complete. The author places a highly significant pericope immediately following this statement which admits failure. In the subsequent incident, the suppliant is carefully identified as "a Greek, a Syro-Phoenician by birth" (7:24). A shift of milieu occurs here: Jesus moves into Gentile territory. The contrast is emphasized by the change of place.

The pericope which follows the failure of the Pharisees and disciples to understand describes the healing of the daughter of a Gentile. The conditions are unusual. The woman dares to speak to a man, a Jewish man at that. She asks healing for her daughter. She manifests how fully she is free from the restraints of law by her action itself, by her request, and in her dialogue with Jesus, the real essence of which is that her heart is free from legal niceties and from any need for self-justification. She is not clinging to any place in society; she simply expects Jesus to heal. She has faith, not in her own value (Jesus compares her to a dog), nor in any observance she might perform, nor in Jewishness, which she did not possess. She has openness of heart and, consequently, she understands. By the placement of this incident, the author has achieved an important irony. The woman, who could have had little or no reason to understand, understands very well, and those who should most certainly have understood do not.

In Chapter 8, verses 14 to 21 contain a final discussion of the total lack of understanding by the disciples, "den dauernden Unverstand der Jünger."[12] Demonstrations of this lack occur again later in the text, but there they occur in actions and without narratorial comment. In the pericope, 8:14–21, the narrator makes it perfectly clear that he is interested in stressing the disciples' inexplicable lack of understanding. He possibly overstresses it.[13] Schweizer writes: "This (verse 15) is the clue which indicates the importance Mark attaches to this misunderstanding by the disciples for which there is no psychological explanation."[14] Mark goes on to elaborate Jesus' severe condemnation of their deficiency through the remaining verses (16–21). He makes it clear that the disciples fail to understand the testimony of their own senses. The motif of misunderstanding is an essential part of the statement being made, that what is to be understood is Jesus' power to feed his people. The lack of understanding is so powerfully expressed that it almost overshadows the larger statement about Jesus at work feeding his people even though that work recalls that God fed his people in the desert in the time of the exodus.

The narrator's voice is used to stress earlier themes such as lack of understanding and hardness of heart. One should note here the almost incomprehensible nature of the question the disciples ask at 8:4: "How can one feed these men with bread here in the desert?" Having experienced the feeding of five thousand from five loaves and two fish, the disciples, again in chorus, dare to ask how anyone can feed four thousand men in the desert. The question is a frank admission that they had completely failed to understand anything at all about the first feeding miracle. The question performs the rhetorical function of stressing the almost unbelievable incomprehension of the disciples. Robert Fowler writes: "Regrettably, many of those who have accurately perceived the author's intended meaning in 8:4 have recoiled from it and have sought to deny it."[15] Perhaps this is a bit overstated, but it certainly helps to establish the intent of 8:4 which is to stress the lack of understanding by the disciples. This theme is recapitulated and developed in 8:14–21.

The irony of 8:14–21 begins with the first words, "They had forgotten to bring bread." One might be allowed to wonder what they had done with the seven baskets gathered up only a few verses earlier. Aside from consideration of form,[16] the saying of verse 15, "Beware of the leaven of the Pharisees and the leaven of Herod," and the verb "cautioned," or perhaps, "gave orders," are a warning not to yield to evil such as that perpetrated by the Pharisees who have asked for a sign (8:11–13). Bratcher describes the leaven as a principle of moral corruption that contaminates all it touches.[17] The disciples enter into discussion with one another but not over the warning against corruption. They miss the point entirely and are concerned only with the sensible reality of the bread. The saying about leaven has been seen by some as totally disjointed from the rest of the pericope.[18] It does not seem necessary to consider it such:

> The figure of leaven thus describes the disposition to believe only if signs which compel faith are produced. In contrast, Jesus' warning constitutes a fresh call to faith and understanding apart from signs.[19]

Taylor also sees it as appropriate in its context: "Mark does not interpret the phrase, but undoubtedly the idea of an evil disposition harmonizes with his story."[20]

From verse 17 to verse 20, Jesus confronts the disciples with the enigma of their lack of understanding about bread. As the Markan author has structured these verses, the two feeding stories follow closely upon each other. Jesus stresses the bread. How could they possibly question about a lack of bread? He asks important questions about perceiving and understanding, about seeing and hearing, as highlighted also in the "opening" passages, 7:31–37; 8:22–26; 8:27–31; 10:46–52. His questions highlight their blindness. They neither perceive the testimony of their own senses nor do they make the obvious judgment about it. This hard-heartedness leads Jesus to a step-by-step dialogue with them as he tries to show them that the testimony of their senses has to be understood in faith. But it *has to be understood* and verse 21 rightly implies that they still do not have the kind of faith that is given to the blind man in the following pericope.

The question remains. How could the disciples not perceive and understand when they had twice participated in these over-abundant multiplyings of bread? The question of what it is they are expected to understand goes, of course, far beyond the production of food. They even lack faith that Jesus can supply their material needs. But more importantly they fail to understand that the multiplication of loaves on two occasions was an act that signified the importance of Jesus' presence among them. They miss the significance of the twelve and seven baskets and, hence, of the abundance and completion of the gift which he brings. The narrator's point of view seems to be that it is all so very obvious that it is incredible that they do not understand.

It seems clear that Mark was interested in the use of numbers. Several possibilities exist for the significance of the numbers used in the feeding narratives. In the earlier story, when five thousand have been fed, twelve baskets of fragments are collected. It has been suggested that the number five thousand is related to the five books of the law while the twelve baskets recall the twelve tribes of Israel and indicate a type of eschatological perfection.[21] The four thousand may be intended to symbolize universality since one thousand often indicates a very large number and four refers to the four corners of the universe as in Isaiah 11:12. The seven baskets gathered up carry the sense of completion and perfection. As hesitant as modern critics must be in attempting to decipher the meanings ancient writers attached to specific numbers, Mark's careful use of them demonstrates that he was in control of his materials and used them for his own purposes.

The author employs contrast to stress the opposite process and hence to accentuate seeing. Some anonymous people bring a blind man to Jesus in Bethsaida. Jesus, step-by-step, opens the eyes of this man until he can see clearly. The contrast is inescapable and ironic.

The parallel texts confirm the fact that the Markan author used this pericope to accentuate the incomprehensible lack of understanding by the disciples. Matthew 16:5–12 carefully subordinates the disciples' lack of understanding to concern about the leaven of the Pharisees and Sadducees. Luke 12:1 includes only the warning against that leaven. Only Mark places the miracle in a context which contrasts it with the lack of understanding by Jesus' chosen disciples.

The disciples are unbraided for their lack of faith in the pericope of 4:35–41. This calming miracle is closely related to the similar narrative in 6:45–52. In both instances Jesus is depicted as bringing deliverance in the same way that God had brought deliverance according to Psalm 65:7–8.

> [God] who dost still the roaring of the seas, the roaring
>   of their waves, the tumult of the peoples, so that
>   those who dwell at earth's farthest bounds are
>   afraid at thy signs.

Robert Fowler points out that "In both sea stories, as well as in both feeding stories, the focus of the action is on the disciples of Jesus."[22]

The first calming is described by all three synoptics: Matthew 8:23–27; Mark 4:35–41; Luke 8:22–25. But Mark differs from Matthew and Luke in two significant ways. Mark uses a series of specific and interesting details: "just as he was" (4:36), "other boats were with him" (4:36), "but he was in the stern asleep on the cushion" (4:38). The presence of these details creates a sense of immediacy and normalcy. Neither Matthew nor Luke includes them.

A second difference from Matthew and Luke is found in Mark's treatment of the request to Jesus. In Matthew the disciples ask, "Save, Lord, we are perishing" (8:25). In Luke they simply describe their plight, "Master, master, we are perishing" (8:24). In Mark they rebuke Jesus and make his lack of action seem a personal affront to them, "Teacher, do you not care if we perish?" (4:38). The disciples, by their great fear, show themselves to be without faith, even to the point of being abusive.

Jesus' conduct gives an example of the type of trust in God described often in the Hebrew scriptures, for example, "I will give peace in the land, and you shall lie down, and none shall make you afraid" (Leviticus 26:6). However, Klausner raises a question about the nature of this event. He labels it "only apparently miraculous."[23] Klausner's concern, of course, is with historicity but his comment raises an important question about the nature of the picture Mark is painting. He bases his point on the fact that storms rise without warning on the Sea of Galilee and disappear just as quickly. The difficulty with this appraisal is found in the words "[he] rebuked the wind, and said to the sea, 'Peace, be still!'" (4:39). The author of Mark seems intent upon establishing a sequence of cause and effect that cannot be ignored. He clearly portrays the action as a miracle. Jesus' rebuke for their lack of faith occurs several additional times in Mark; cf. 7:14–23; 8:14–21; 8:31–33.

All three synoptic accounts conclude the story of the calming of the sea with the rhetorical question, "Who, then, is this?" (4:41). Fowler writes:

> This concluding, unanswered, rhetorical question is doubly important for the reader of the gospel. First, it reveals to the reader that the disciples have not even begun to fathom this person whom they call "teacher" in their time of peril (4:38). At the same time, the unanswered question stands as a guidepost for the reader, indicating in the starkest possible manner the central question addressed by Mark's gospel: "Who then is this . . . ?"[24]

The expected answer should have been, at the very least, that Jesus is someone who has done what the God of Israel had done for his people.

The second calming story, in 6:45–52, depends more upon Jesus as a person than the first one did. He comes to his disciples walking on the sea. There are no challenges, no requests, no rebukes. The point of the narrative seems to be the statement made in verse 52, "for they did not understand about the loaves, but their hearts were hardened." The ultimate cause of their failure to understand follows, that is, their hardness of heart.[25]

The Disciples Fail

Jesus' final failure with his disciples is recorded in the narrative between the end of the Passover meal (14:31), and the trial before Pilate beginning at 15:1. Judas betrays Jesus (14:1–2; 14:10–11; 14:43–50). The device of intercalation is used to intrude the contrasting story of the woman at Bethany (14:3–9) within the two parts of the betrayal scene (14:1–2 and 14:10–11).

The treachery of Judas and the hatred of the officials is contrasted with the courage and generosity of the woman who anointed Jesus' body. The economy of verses 10–11 should be noted. No motivation for Judas' action is given. No details of how or why are given. The amount of money is not specified. The verb exētoun is used of the officials in verse 1, "who were seeking to arrest him by stealth" and of Judas who (exētai) "sought an opportunity to betray him" in verse 11. It is the same verb which was used of his family in 3:32, of the chief priests and scribes in 11:18 and 12:12. The author often associates seeking with opposition.

The treachery of Judas' action is accentuated by his greeting as "Master," and by the kiss which was a normal way for a disciple to greet his rabbi.[26] The narrator stresses the element of treachery by depicting the crowd "from the chief priests, and the scribes and the elders" (14:43); by the detail with which the kiss is described and by the failure of Jesus to give any attention to the slave who had lost an ear. This narrator's portrayal stresses Judas as betrayer, the humiliation heaped upon Jesus by the manner of his arrest, and the final ignominy of 14:50 when the disciples all flee. In such manner Judas' treachery is seen as only the most blatant example of the failure of all the disciples.

In the pericope which preceded Jesus' arrest (14:32–42) the three disciples, Peter, James and John, were singled out for a special revelation:

> Peter, James and John are chosen to be present as they were earlier selected to witness Jesus' power over death and the epiphany of his eschatological glory. The singling out of the three at Gethsemane, therefore, signifies the importance of what transpires there, as conversely their lack of performance raises the issue of failure in leadership.[27]

They have seen Jesus transfigured in glory. They are now afforded the chance to see him overwhelmed with sorrow in Gethsemane. Questions of historicity aside, the narrative serves two obvious ends: to depict the struggle of Jesus in his final hours and to illustrate the growing confusion, lack of commitment, and pure selfishness on the part of Peter and his companions. Jesus is in mortal, even cosmic, struggle and his chosen disciples sleep, not once, but three times. The first part of the pericope, verses 32–36, concerns itself totally with Jesus in solitary prayer. At verse 37 the emphasis changes completely from Jesus' struggle to the failure of the disciples. The direction changes again with the words, "It is enough," words found only in Mark. The first failure of the disciples in the final hour has occurred. It will be followed immediately by more serious failures. More so than Matthew or Luke, Mark stresses Jesus' consciousness that he has failed to win over the disciples:

> Jesus overcomes his desire not to drink the cup (cf. 14:36) and the disciples evade drinking from the cup. In a sense all remains the same as before. With Gethsemane the conflict between Jesus and the disciples has been brought to a head and proven insoluble.[28]

Peter's denial in 14:66–72 depicts Jesus' final failure with the disciples. The synoptic accounts are basically the same. The important aspects seem to be that Peter's accuser is only a serving maid, that Peter denies knowing Jesus three separate times, and that the crowing of the cock reminds Peter that Jesus had prophesied this event. Its importance as prophecy has already been noted.[29] Peter's cowardice is stressed by the fact that a mere maid accuses him. In Mark alone is added the detail that Peter was warming himself by the fire. Peter's protestations grow in intensity with each repetition. Tannehill believes that "the narrative goes into unnecessary detail, recording three separate denials and building to a climax with the third, which is accompanied by a curse."[30] The disciples who had failed to keep vigil in Gethesmane, and who had fled from the scene of the arrest, are now further typified in Peter who vehemently denies any knowledge of Jesus. The final mention of the disciples in Mark (with the exception of the message sent to them in 16:7) is of Peter weeping at his own failure. Regardless of any other purpose of this narrative of denial (it surely has several), it brings full circle the failure of Jesus to establish a group of faithful disciples.

Béda Rigaux has pointed out the fact that,

> Nul d'ailleurs plus que Marc n'a uni Jésus à ses disciples. Mt. et Luc omettant de les mentionner dans des endroits parallèles à ceux de Mc.[31]

> And again: Mt. dans 7 cas et Lc dans 8 cas ont omis la mention des disciples pour ne plus mentionner que Jésus.[32]

It is impossible to deny the fact that Mark's portrait emphasizes and ends with total failure on the part of the disciples. Modern writers have explained away the failure in a variety of ways. Weeden, for example, writes that the disciples had clung to a divine-man christology and that to Mark this constituted heresy. Meye writes that the humanness of the twelve brings about their failure but the fact that they remain chosen ones shows divine action in overcoming their failure. Hawkin asserts that what the disciples fail to comprehend is mystery. He calls the incomprehension of the disciples a "typology per contrarium" which is the result of Jesus contradicting their human desires and ambitions.[33] Hawkin's work has the important value that it treats the incomprehension as a negative that is not subsumed. It does not explore the implications of that finding. However, there is no way to change the basically negative orientation of this portrait. As Achtemeier has written:

> Time and again, despite private explanations (4:10, 34; 7:17; 9:28; 10:10), they betray their inability to grasp what is going on about them (e.g. 4:13; 6:52; 7:18; 8:17; 9:32). They say things that show their total lack of comprehension of what Jesus tried to tell them (e.g. 8:32; 10:38), and they confirm their failure when in the critical moment they all desert him. They have thus not only misunderstood, they have rejected what they have seen.[34]

Since the disciples, as a group, disappear totally at 14:50 and Peter does the same at 14:72, the breakdown is total. The author has treated the disciples in a manner similar to that which he used with Jesus' family. Jesus had failed with his disciples as he had failed with his family and neighbors and as he had failed at the very beginning with those this author believed represented official Judaism. No relief from this picture of failure is provided.

Failure with Family and Neighbors

Most authors who are seriously engaged in portraying a successful personage find it helpful to begin with a description of his relationships to those closest to him, that is, to his family, friends and neighbors. Glowing stories of an unusual birth and wondrous feats performed as a youth would be very much in order. Most certainly models for such usage are plentiful in ancient literature. Writings such as Plutarch's *Lives*[35] use the technique extensively. A specific example can be found in Philo's *On Moses*.[36] Matthew and Luke both realized the value of such stories and used them in their first chapters.[37] Mark did not use such stories.

Omission of Birth Narratives

Birth narratives which glorify parents and child were often used in the effort to enhance the stature of the subject of the life. For example, Diogenes Laertius, in *Lives of the Eminent Philosophers* (3:1–2), describes the birth of Plato as miraculous and fixes the date according to the procedures of the time.[38] And, in Plutarch's *Parallel Lives*, Alexander 2:1–3:2, it is proposed that Alexander's mother "had conceived him through the agency of one of the gods, namely Zeus."[39] The narrator of Mark's gospel makes no effort to glorify Jesus by birth narratives nor by the description of extraordinary exploits performed while he was growing up. This would seem to have been a conscious omission, all the more so since the portrayal of the family is so negative in Chapters 3 and 6. The Markan author knew something of Jesus' origins, "Is not this the carpenter, the son of Mary and brother of James and Moses and Judas and Simon?" (6:3). He chose not to include any details or narratives of Jesus' birth and early years. Mark's narrative begins "in media res" where adulation is shared with

John the Baptizer. The parallels, of course, are significantly different:

> Matthew and Luke saw Christological implications in stories that were in circulation about Jesus' birth; or, at least, they saw the possibility of weaving such stories into a narrative of their own composition. . . . [40]

Evidently, Mark did not.

By the time that he chooses to introduce Jesus' family in 3:20–21, the narrator has already sketched the main outlines of his portrait of Jesus. The narrator and the reader both know that Jesus has been proclaimed Messiah and Son of God (1:1), that a voice has proclaimed him beloved Son (1:11), that unclean spirits have recognized him (1:24). They also know that he has performed deeds consonant with such an exalted state. He has called disciples, taught, driven out unclean spirits, healed, and aggravated the religious establishment. This is summarized in 3:7–12.

Jesus at Home

The call of twelve disciples immediately precedes Jesus' going home (3:20),[41] where his first interaction with his family occurs. The placement of the call narrative provides a sharp contrast with the behavior and attitudes of the family. The list of disciples is detached and even mechanical:

> A catalogue which includes proper names, a patrronymic, surnames and by-names, which omits Levi, and contains terms like Boanerges and Iscariot, strange perhaps already to Mark himself, is hardly the kind of thing the Evangelist would have constructed if he had been writing freely.[42]

Nonetheless, the list provides valuable clues to the attitude of Jesus toward his disciples. It is prefaced with the expression, "those whom he desired" (3:13). It continues that he appointed these disciples "to be with him, and to be sent out to preach and have authority to cast out demons" (3:14–15). These men were called to participate in Jesus' ministry and to form a permanent group with whom he desired to live. They would seem to constitute his real family. This suspicion is confirmed at the end of Chapter 3, "Here are my mother and my brothers" (3:34).

The fact that Jesus' family and his disciples are treated differently is obvious in the opening words of each incident. At verse 13, Jesus had gone up into the hills. At verse 20, "he went home." The twelve who had been with him in the hills are not mentioned in the verses about his family. Jesus had been proclaimed Son of God in 3:11 and recognized as charismatic leader in 3:13–19. In verses 20 and 21 there is a sharp contrast, as Nineham has noted:

> The first verse (19b) re-emphasizes what has been shown in the previous passage (vv. 71-9a)—that ordinary, unprejudiced folk, recognizing (we may assume) the goodness and Godgiven character of Jesus' power, flocked to avail themselves of it. In the rest of the section we are shown by contrast how those who might have been expected to share this attitude to the full, Jesus' own family and the religious leaders of the people, not only failed to recognize the true source and character of his actions, but insisted on attributing them to evil sources.[43]

At this juncture, his family is said to have thought him mad (exestē). Klausner describes what may be the import of the family's concern:

> His miracles did not inspire them with a belief in him: they simply looked upon them as the tricks of an eccentric and "wonderworker," familiar to the Galilee of that time and in the East generally.[44]

At this point, the narrator introduces the representatives of official Judaism who repeat what is, in essence, the same charge his family has made. In this manner he makes his point that Jesus' own, his family and his people, consider him possessed.

There is a subtle distinction made between the true Israel recalled by the naming of the twelve, and official Israel represented by the scribes who are carefully described as having come "down from Jerusalem" (3:22). These scribes may represent official Judaism and in this gospel they do just that, but they are, literally at least, contrasted with the twelve disciples who may be intended to represent the twelve tribes and thus the true Israel.

In support of the contention that the author of Mark chose negation as a tool in his description of Jesus is the fact that verses 20 and 21 are found neither in Matthew nor in Luke. There is nothing even similar to them in the other synoptics. Only Mark places Jesus in clear conflict with his family.

The remainder of the chapter seems to be structured as an intercalation or, as Neirynck prefers, "a sandwich arrangement."[45] Verses 22–30 deal with the continuing controversy with the scribes. As has been seen,[46] there is a close connection between the charge made by the family and that made by the scribes. However, only verses 20–21 and 31–35 deal directly with Jesus' family. This family is identified as hoi par' autou in verse 21. The translation of that phrase as family has the weight of scholarship behind it.[47] The fact that his mother and his brothers are the focus of the final verse of the section adds to the likelihood that "family" is the correct translation.

His family members go out to seize him. The strong phrase kratēsai auton introduces the startling charge that Jesus is beside himself, another way of saying that he is mad. The charge is essentially the same as the one the scribes make, that he is possessed by Beelzebub. The meaning is so clear as to be indisputable. Trocmé writes:

> In fact, the author of Mark does mean that Jesus' family accused him of being mad and, seeing him installed at a distance with his disciples and followed by a great crowd, they set out on an expedition to take hold of him and bring him back.[48]

There seems no other possible reason for the inclusion of this passage in this narrative than to stress the failure of Jesus to influence his family and his family's total failure to understand him. The charge is shocking, clearly too shocking for Matthew and Luke. It is the kind of accusation that would never be found in a laudatory biography. It is even without good motivation since the reason for their concern seems to have been that crowds surrounding Jesus were so large that Jesus and his disciples could not eat. Admittedly the reference to "they" is ambiguous but, whatever the antecedent, the presence of large crowds is hardly adequate reason for considering someone mad.

Verses 22 to 30 intercalate another conflict story, this one with scribes. This serves as a reminder that opposition to Jesus is continuing. It also reminds the reader, by association, of the rejection of Jesus by the officials.

The final pericope of this section, verses 31–35, is the second part of the family incident.[49] It completes the contrast between those who reject Jesus, that is, his family and the scribes (3:20–21), and those who follow him, that is, an unidentified crowd (3:20) and a special twelve, eight of whom have not been heard of before in this gospel (3:13–19).

At verse 31, Jesus' mother and brothers come to call him. The time and place are not mentioned nor are proper names given. The interest is not biographical. Only two things are important. Obedience to God's will is essential and only that constitutes true kinship with Jesus. His mother and his brothers belong to the group that is outside, who are not granted full revelation lest they believe (4:11-12). That they remain outside, that they summon Jesus to come outside, that they intend to carry him away, are all indications that they are doing their own will and are far from doing the will of God.

The crowd choruses to Jesus that his mother and his brothers are outside and that they seek him. The verb for seek, zētousin, is used eight times in Mark. In 1:37, 8:11 and here in 3:32, it means to look for. However, in 11:18, 12:12, 14:1, 14:11 and 14:55 it means to look for in order to destroy or kill. Here it certainly means to look for, but it may also imply a desire to apprehend or even to destroy. The effect is disquieting, especially in a passage which contains the charge that he is mad and in which his family is said to be outside.

The capstone of the pericope is the rhetorical question of verse 33, "Who are my mother and my brothers?" The literal answer to the question is so obvious that there must be another meaning. The question constitutes a radical disowning of the family that accuses Jesus in the same manner that the scribes accuse him. He is not asking if his mother and brothers are standing outside. He is asking what characterizes true membership in his family. In the final verse Jesus answers his own question. Human bonds and family relationships are less significant, in fact meaningless, without obedience to God. Jesus' family is willing to believe that he is possessed by an unclean spirit. This calls into question their relationship with God.

So, the section which began with the ironic situation of the unclean spirits proclaiming Jesus Son of God (3:11), while his own countrymen look for miracles (3:10), closes with the declaration that no bond of relationship to Jesus is of any value unless it involves personal fellowship in doing the will of God. Those who should be closest to Jesus are "outside" and even the amorphous crowd is closer than they. This provides the reader with some insight into the narrator's point of view. Shocking as it may be, Jesus' family has rejected him. He has been a failure with his own people. As Lane has summarized:

> By following Jesus the Twelve are marked off as those who do the will of God. Jesus' statement regarding the true family, however, looks beyond the Twelve to a larger company of men and women: "*whoever* shall do the will of God is my brother, and sister, and mother."[50]

The Prophet without Honor

The final incident involving Jesus' family occurs in 6:1–6. In the same chapter, verses 7–13 bring to a close the commissioning of disciples. The two pericopae form a parallel to 3:13–19 and 3:20–35. The theme of rejection by those who have most reason to understand Jesus is contrasted in Chapter 3 with the call of the twelve to be Jesus' true family. The same structure occurs in Chapter 6. In the first pericope, Jesus' own reject him. In the second, he sends out the twelve, who successfully share in his power of preaching, exorcising and healing.

In the first six verses, attention focuses on his own who do not know him. They are found in the synagogue on the sabbath much as the audience in 1:21–28. In Chapter 6 the problem of Jesus' relatives is somewhat different from that faced by them in Chapter 3. There the only complaint they seem to have is that Jesus and his followers do not have time to eat. In Chapter 6 there are three specific areas with which they are concerned: his teaching, his wisdom and his mighty works. None of these seems terribly subversive. However, the increasing intensity of tone from verse 2 to verse 3 dramatizes the progressive hostility.

Martin Hengel has pointed out the literary skill with which this pericope was constructed:

> Mark 6:1–6, the outright rejection in Nazareth, is an
> important turning point; in this pericope Mark very skill-
> fully introduces all the necessary biographical details
> about Jesus' profession and family which we did not have
> in the brief introduction of Jesus in 1:9.[51]

The narrator recounts that Jesus came to his own country. The word patrida carries two related meanings, something like hometown as well as fatherland. Both meanings are appropriate in this verse. As Kelber notes, the author's concern is not with the town of Nazareth: "It was not the town of Nazareth as much as it was Jesus' next of kin, his house and family that provoked him to make the break."[52] Jesus is among his own relatives and in his own home, but he is also, in a symbolic way, experiencing rejection by all of his own. The disciples who had followed him (6:1) are present but play no part in the action. Their presence foreshadows the commissioning in the next pericope and serves as a reminder that a comparison is involved. However, the disciples here, as elsewhere, are not a well-defined group. They seem to be all the followers who are with Jesus on this journey.

Verse 2 recalls 1:21–22 in form, content and vocabulary. In Chapter 1, Jesus is in Capernaum with his four newly called disciples. It is the sabbath. He teaches in the synagogue. They are all astonished (exeplēssanto). In Chapter 6, Jesus is in his own country with disciples. It is again the sabbath. He teaches in the synagogue and many are astonished (exeplēssonto). There seems to be ironic intent in the choice of vocabulary for verses 2 and 3, tauta, sophia, dunameis and toi autoi. The tone of "Where did this man get all this?", the implications of his exercising wisdom, the magnitude of mighty deeds, especially "such as these," all carry an irony close to sarcasm. By verse 3, the tone has become openly hostile: "Is not this the carpenter?" and "they took offense at him."

The astonished, or hostile, in verses 2 and 3 ask important questions. They are the right questions. They want to know who Jesus is and where he came from. They want to know by what power he can do mighty deeds. They are proper questions which could lead to correct understandings of Jesus' identity. However, the narrator chooses to use a tone which changes honest inquiry into derogatory belittling at the hands of Jesus' own kindred.

The exact meaning, and even the text of verse 3, have been the matter of extensive controversy. However, the difficulty of the two forms is resolved; whether ho tektōn ho huios tēs Marias or tou tektovos huios kai Marias is correct,[53] some elements are clear. The words "son of Mary" do not appear anywhere else in the gospels or epistles. It is possible that the author did not realize that Jewish men were not identified through their mothers, or that this usage simply indicates that his father was no longer living, but it is difficult to believe that three consecutive statements that seem to belittle could have been unintentional. Jesus is called carpenter (ho tektōn) and therefore without teaching, wisdom or ability to perform great works.[54] He is called "son of Mary" which could have been an insult.[55] He is identified as one of a family which is lowly and insignificant just as the speakers are. Jesus' own reject him precisely because he is their own and therefore cannot be anyone important. They do not want to believe in him because they are humble and insignificant. They are even scandalized because he is one of them. The point could hardly be clearer. Jesus' own reject him because he has no right to be better than they are. Here, in the final encounter of Jesus with his family, one reason for the lack of understanding emerges. The prophet and teacher they follow will have to be someone different from themselves and not someone who appears as a poor, itinerant preacher who works some wonders. They have hardened their hearts to one of their own who claims to be more than they are. A significant part of this negative portrayal of Jesus' relationship with his relatives is the omission of these relatives from the rest of the narrative.

Jesus responds to their having taken offense by using what Bultmann calls a *secular mashal* made into a *dominical saying:*[56] "A prophet is not without honor, except in his own country, among his own kin, and in his own house" (6:4). The last two phrases, "among his own kin" and "in his own house," seem to be additions to an original saying.[57] They emphasize the identity of those who are unconvinced.

Possibly Jesus' attribution of the word "prophet" to himself is ironic. There is no mention of his having prophesied or having been accused of such before this moment. Verse 5 tells how it had become impossible for him to work there. Mark's purpose seems to be to stress the inability of these people to hear, even if a prophet were to speak.

Verse 5 includes the very difficult clause, "he could do no mighty work there." Scholars have struggled to explain this claim to lack of ability on Jesus' part. "It is a frank admission of Jesus' dependence upon those he wished to serve."[58] "Jesus falls out of the power of the Spirit."[59] "Jesus seems to have thought of faith as a natural attitude."[60] "Jesus was not unable but not free to do it in these circumstances."[61] "His refusal was one of protest."[62] Nonetheless, the text states that Jesus was *not able* to do any mighty work there. One notable exception is made, however. He did heal some sick. No reason is offered for the selective healings. The unbelief of Jesus' family, friends and neighbors was so great that it cut off Jesus' work, but it would seem that the narrator does not want to cut Jesus off completely. Jesus continues to perform compassionate acts but, at the same time, Mark wants to make the point that Jesus' neighbors were scandalized by him. Again, as in 1:29–31, healings seem to have taken place on the sabbath and no objections are raised.

The passage ends with the unusual comment, "And he marveled because of their unbelief" (6:6a). This is the only place in Mark's account where Jesus is said to have "marveled" (ethaumazon); the word occurs three other times in Mark: the residents of the Decapolis, "all men marveled" (ethaumazon) (5:20); Pilate wondered (thaumazein) at Jesus' refusal to respond to the charges brought against him (15:5); again, Pilate wondered (ethaumasen) if Jesus had, indeed, died (15:44). In all of these usages, the most apparent meaning is pondering deeply with some surprise. Jesus is misunderstood by most of the participants in this story. Only of his family's disbelief is it recorded that he pondered it deeply and was somewhat surprised by it.

Matthew's account (13:54–58) centers around the slightly more moderate effect that "they took offense at him" (13:57). There is only a suggestion of conflict in the narrative. Those present ask if Jesus is not the carpenter's son and if his mother is not called Mary. The derogatory implications are missing. Matthew's final verse adds that "he did not do many mighty works there," not that he could not. Matthew does not have the intensifying comment that Mark adds, "he marveled because of their unbelief" (6:6a).

Luke's account is significantly different (4:16–30). The synagogue-goers recognize Jesus as *Joseph's* son after he has explained an Isaian passage for them. Their antagonism results in an effort to kill Jesus, but their motivation is unclear. At verse 22 they are marveling at his graciousness and speaking well of him. Immediately thereafter, in verses 23 and 24, Jesus begins to explain the lack of acceptance experienced by the prophets. There is no mention of belief or of failure to believe but there is mention of a serious effort to kill Jesus (29–30). Matthew's version seems an almost reluctant admission that Jesus' relatives did not believe in him. Luke makes the narrative into a mixed story of acceptance and rejection. Only Mark treats the incident with the direct and total rejection of Jesus by his family and friends in the midst of a hostile encounter. Mark, alone, accentuates the rejection of Jesus by his own.

Many elements stress the contrast between the commissioning of the twelve and the rejection by Jesus' relatives. The placement of the two pericopae is the first and most obvious. The structure of verses 6 and 7a provides a seam which permits the separation of the two pericopae but also maintains the narrative flow. Verse 6 has two independent clauses which almost constitute a statement of cause and effect. Jesus was amazed that they did not believe and then he went among the villages teaching. This flows into the third clause, 7a, "he called to him the twelve." These verses are economical and loosely parallel. In each clause (the first two are sentences), kai is followed by a finite verb and a modifying phrase. The meaning adds progression and suggestion of causality to the parallel—he marveled at their belief, then he left, then he called his disciples. Jesus is in awe at their unbelief and probably at their reason for not believing. He goes out to teach. This fact is related with no embellishment, no adornment, no development. It moves Jesus away from "his own house." He calls the twelve who have been called before (3:13–19). Previously they were called just before he was rejected; this time they are called just after the rejection. The author arranges his material to stress again the great irony of Jesus' rejection by those who had most reason to accept him. This is contrasted with the belief of the twelve who, at this point at least, share in his teaching and healing.

Relatively early in his account, Mark has placed Jesus' family in total hostility to him. Jesus has failed completely to bring them to belief, to inspire them to follow him, to honor him in any way. Vernon Robbins, in his discussion of the formal structure of Mark, writes:

> The confusion and anger expressed by the scribes and Pharisees (2:1–3:6), the lack of understanding expressed by Jesus' mother and brothers (3:21, 31–35), and the request by the Gerasenes that Jesus go away from their neighborhood (5:17), prepare the reader for the negative reception of Jesus in his homeland (6:1–3). In the midst of a logical progression that arose from the plan to destroy Jesus, a qualitative progression occurs in which the negative responses to Jesus are accepted by Jesus as an important

aspect of his identity. He is not only appropriately called Son of God but also appropriately called "a prophet without honor."[63]

Jesus' separation from his own is final. The family does not appear again in Mark's account. They are not mentioned as being present at the trial, at the crucifixion, burial or among those who go out and find the empty tomb. The rejection is never rescinded, is never softened. The omission of the family from the second part of the narrative adds to the over-all pattern of rejection. Mark portrays Jesus' family, friends and neighbors as totally and finally unbelieving.

The irony of this series of events is both dramatic and contextual. The reader and the narrator are well informed of who Jesus is. Those closest to him are not. The strangers he has called to follow him are described as "those whom he desired" (3:13), and they are told: "to you has been given the secret of the kingdom of God" (4:11). On the other hand, Jesus is forced to marvel at the unbelief of "his own kin" and "those in his own house" (6:4–6a). Those who know him best actually know him least, think him mad and are condemned to remain "outside." His own reject him because he is their own.

NOTES

[1]Some examples, J.B. Tyson, "The Blindness of the Disciples in Mark," *JBL* 80 (1961): 261–268. David J. Hawkin, "The Incomprehension of the Disciples in the Marcan Redaction," *JBL* 91 (1972): 491–500 et al.

[2]Robert C. Tannehill, "The Disciples in Mark: The Function of a Narrative Role," *JR* 57 (1977): 403.

[3]Achtemeier, *Mark*, p. 92.

[4]Trocmé, *Formation of the Gospel according to Mark*, p. 142.

[5] Cranfield, *The Gospel according to Mark*, p. 227. See also Nineham, *Saint Mark*, p. 180. E. Schweizer, *The Good News according to Mark*, trans. D. Madvig (Richmond: John Knox Press, 1970). p. 141. Hooker, *The Message of Mark*, p. 44.

[6] Achtemeier, *Mark*, p. 95.

[7] Johnson, *The Gospel according to St. Mark*, p. 128.

[8] Robinson, *The Problem of History in Mark*, p. 76.

[9] Ibid.

[10] Schweizer, *The Good News according to Mark*, p. 147.

[11] See above, Chapter 4.

[12] Erich Klostermann, *Das Markusevangelium* (Mohr: Tübingen, 1971). p. 77.

[13] Taylor, *The Gospel according to St. Mark*, p. 367.

[14] Schweizer, *The Good News according to Mark*, p. 160.

[15] Fowler, *Loaves and Fishes*, p. 96.

[16] Bultmann, *The History of the Synoptic Tradition*, p. 331.

[17] Robert G. Bratcher and Eugene A. Neda, *A Translator's Handbook on the Gospel of Mark* (London: United Bible Societies, 1961), p. 253.

[18] Bultmann, *The History of the Synoptic Tradition*, p. 331 and Lohmeyer, *Das Evangelium des Markus*, p. 157 et al.

[19] Lane, *Commentary on the Gospel of Mark*, p. 281.

[20] Taylor, *The Gospel according to St. Mark*, p. 365.

[21] Nineham, *Saint Mark*, p. 207.

[22] Fowler, *Loaves and Fishes*, p. 101.

[23] Klausner, *Jesus of Nazareth*, p. 269.

[24] Ibid.

[25] See above in this chapter.

[26] Lane, *Commentary on the Gospel of Mark*, p. 525.

[27] Werner H. Kelber, "The Hour of the Son of Man and the Temptation of the Disciples," in Werner H. Kelber, *The Passion in Mark* (Philadelphia: Fortress, 1976), p. 47.

[28] Kelber, "The Hour of the Son of Man and the Temptation of the Disciples," p. 54.

[29] See above, Chapter 4.

[30] Tannehill, "The Disciples in Mark: The Function of a Narrative Role," p. 403.

[31] Béda Rigaux, *Témoignage de l'évangile de Marc* (Bruges: Desclée de Brouwer, 1965), p. 157.

[32] Ibid. p. 158.

[33] Theodore J. Weeden, *Traditions in Conflict*. (Philadelphia: Fortress, 1971), pp. 159–160. Meye, *Jesus and the Twelve*, p. 211 and p. 224. Hawkin, "The Incomprehension of the Disciples in the Markan Redaction," p. 500.

[34] Achtemeier, *Mark*, p. 93.

[35] Plutarch, *The Parallel Lives*, Eng. trans. B. Perrin, Vols. 1–10, Loeb Classical Library (Cambridge: Harvard University Press, 1960).

[36] Philo, *On Moses*, Eng. trans. F.H. Colson, Vol. 6, Loeb Classical Library (Cambridge: Harvard University Press, 1966).

[37] Matthew 1 and 2 and Luke 1 and 2.

[38] Cartlidge, *Documents for the Study of the Gospels*, p. 129.

[39] Ibid. p. 131.

[40] Raymond E. Brown, *The Birth of the Messiah* (New York: Doubleday, 1977), p. 29.

[41] These are the opening words of verse 20 in Nestle-Aland and *The New American Bible*. They are the closing words of verse 19 in Westcott and Hort, *RSV* and *Oxford Annotated Bible*.

[42] Taylor, *The Gospel according to St. Mark*, p. 229.

[43] Nineham, *Saint Mark*, p. 119.

[44] Klausner, *Jesus of Nazareth*, p. 260.

[45] Neirynck, *Duality in Mark*, p. 133.

[46] See above, Chapter 4.

[47] Zerwick, *A Grammatical Analysis of the Greek New Testament*, p. 109. Taylor, *The Gospel according to Mark*, p. 236 et al.

[48]Trocmé, *Formation of the Gospel according to Mark,* p. 134.

[49]Taylor, *The Gospel according to St. Mark,* p. 245. Trocmé, *Formation of the Gospel according to Mark,* p. 82. Bultmann, *The History of the Synoptic Tradition,* p. 29.

[50]Lane, *Commentary on the Gospel of Mark,* p. 248.

[51]Martin Hengel, *Studies in the Gospel of Mark* (Philadelphia: Fortress, 1985), p. 35.

[52]Kelber, *The Kingdom in Mark,* p. 54.

[53]Nestle-Aland, *Novum Testamentum Graece,* p. 105. Metzger, *A Textual Commentary on the Greek New Testament,* pp. 88–89.

[54]Klausner, *Jesus of Nazareth,* p. 235. Taylor, *The Gospel according to St. Mark,* p. 300. Lane, *Commentary on the Gospel of Mark,* p. 202.

[55]C.E.B. Cranfield, *The Gospel according to St. Mark* (Cambridge: Cambridge University Press, 1959). For a complete discussion see Raymond E. Brown, *The Birth of the Messiah* (New York: Doubleday, 1977), pp. 537–541.

[56]Bultmann, *The History of the Synoptic Tradition,* p. 102.

[57]Ibid. p. 31.

[58]Moule, *The Gospel according to Mark,* p. 47.

[59]Robinson, *The Problem of History in Mark,* p. 70.

[60]Taylor, *The Gospel according to St. Mark,* p. 301.

[61]Lane, *Commentary on the Gospel of Mark,* p. 204.

[62]Schmid, *The Gospel according to Mark,* p. 118.

[63]Robbins, *Jesus the Teacher,* p. 37.

Chapter 6

FURTHER EVIDENCE

Limited Arguments

There is evidence of negation in Mark's gospel which is strong but less definitive than the arguments about John the Baptizer and the various groups who fail to understand Jesus. This evidence adds strength to the thesis of a level of negation. These arguments may be less definitive because they are concentrated in a small part of the narrative or because they involve significant omissions, and the argument from silence is never quite as strong as the argument from evidence. Some concern themselves with devices used to affect the tone or direction of a narrative.

There are four arguments which may be considered less definitive evidence. Two of them revolve around the final chapter, the empty tomb narrative. The lack of resurrection narratives and the enigmas in the eight verses of chapter 16 add significantly to the effect of negation. In a real way they bring this level to a conclusion. The treatment of miracles and the author's practice of limiting witnesses furnish still further evidence.

Two related but separate problems arise from the nature of the final chapter. The first question involves the very nature of the eight verses. The second can be stated quite simply. Why did this writer choose not to include stories of resurrection appearances? If resurrection narratives were available, and it seems safe to assume that they were,[1] any sort of biography tending toward the *encomium* type would include such narratives. They would furnish just the kind of supernatural vindication that the writer of a life of Jesus would relish. It seems quite probable then that the author of Mark *chose* not to include resurrection narratives. One entirely logical explanation of such a choice is that this author did not intend to write an *encomium* or anything approximating it. The final chapter is in keeping with this resolve.

The second argument concerns the highly enigmatic nature of the empty tomb narrative in 16:1–8. This final chapter has been the subject of extensive research and speculation.[2] Because verse 8 is so abrupt, because it ends with ephobounto gar, and because the implications of the women's actions are so startling, many students of the Markan gospel have found this ending problematic and even forbidding. Study of the whole empty tomb narrative (16:1–8) adds to the difficulty of understanding the final verse. There is ample evidence that the ending has always been seen as problematic because there are several variant readings proposed in the translations and in the Greek manuscripts.[3] Later authors, evidently made uncomfortable by the abruptness of 16:8, provided resurrection narratives to complete the gospel.[4] William R. Farmer, among contemporary authors, argues for the authenticity of Mark 16:9–20.[5] Nonetheless, most recent scholarship tends toward the conviction that the gospel ends at 16:8 and that this ending provides a fitting conclusion to the text.[6]

R.H. Lightfoot examined the various arguments generally used to explain this unusual ending:

a. the author had intended to proceed farther, but was prevented from doing so, whether by death or some other reason;
b. the author did proceed farther, but at a very early date, all that he wrote after 16:8 was lost;
c. the author ended his work intentionally at 16:8.[7]

Lightfoot's conclusion that a. and b. are speculative and that c. is the most reasonable explanation is accepted by most scholars today. However, Bultmann maintains that the second proposition is "by no means as incomprehensible as E. Meyer maintains."[8] Nineham accepts the third conclusion but with some hesitation.[9] More recent writers tend to accept without reservation Lightfoot's third conclusion. This provides a starting point for discussion of the pericope.

It seems possible, then, to assume that 16:8 is the final verse of Mark's gospel and was intended by the author to be such. It is consequent upon this assumption that the author of the gospel chose not to include some narratives which support the affirmative level of the presentation of Jesus, that is, stories of resurrection appearances. It also seems valid to conclude that the narrative in Mark ends intentionally with a negative component.

Discussion of the narrative of 16:1–8 has revolved around a variety of significant topics, such as its relationship with the "resurrection apparition" of 6:45–52,[10] the possible historicity of the presence of the women,[11] the "interruption" which the command to move into Galilee embodies,[12] and the theological polemic some see as the purpose of the narrative.[13] The negative elements of the story have recently come under close scrutiny,[14] even to the point of the postulating of an hypothesis that there is an apparent effort to create an "anti-tradition of the ET (Empty Tomb). On earth there are no apparitions but only the harsh negative of the ET and the Lord who 'is not here.'"[15] The present examination will concern itself with those negative elements of the story which can be observed in four examples: the three difficulties concerning the women; the empty tomb itself; the emotional responses of the women and their flight; the over-all significance of the final verse.

There are three distinct difficulties involved in Mark's conception of the women's early morning errand. They go out to find Jesus' body, they wish to anoint this body for burial and they are concerned about having someone to roll back the stone for them. The historical and logical difficulties with these details, such as the immense difficulty of removing the stone which sealed the tomb and the extreme unlikelihood that anyone would want to anoint a body which had been in the tomb for thirty-six hours, are not concerns of this study. However, the narrative problems are. Bultmann has pointed out:

> His [Mark's] construction is impressive: the wondering of the women v. 3, the surprised sight of the rolled away stone and the appearance of the angel v. 4ff., the masterly formulated angelic message v. 6 and the shattering impression of v. 8.[16]

Part of the mastery is the author's presentation of the women as, humanly speaking, wrong on all three counts of their purpose: to roll back the stone, to find the body and to anoint it. Their very going out to find the body means that they did not understand what Jesus had taught. Their eyes tell them that the stone had been rolled away, but no attempt is made to explain how it came to be so. The young man tells them that Jesus is not to be found where they are looking. It is difficult to believe that the women "who came up with him to Jerusalem" (15:41) would not have known about the anointing of Jesus' body by the woman at Bethany or about his announcement that she had done it for his burial (14:8). The women came for three reasons; they are wrong on all three. They have not understood.

Mark concentrates on the failure of the women. The impression is inescapable that they understand nothing of what has occurred. It is not so in Matthew's account (28:1–20). Supernatural phenomena occur there: an earthquake and two angels who appear like lightning. The guards are the ones to be afraid (Matthew 28:2–4). The message and the commission to the disciples are much the same as in Mark's account, but the women leave "with fear and great joy" (28:8) and run to tell the disciples. The Lukan writer describes two men in "dazzling apparel" (Luke 24:4). The message they deliver is really an announcement of the fulfillment of the passion-resurrection predictions (9:24; 9:44; 18:32). The women go into the tomb and find it empty without any help from the messengers. They then return to the eleven and deliver the message. Those who hear the message do not believe (Luke 24:11) but the women have fulfilled their charge adequately. Clearly, Mark's concentration on the failure of the women is different from Matthew's stress on the supernatural occurrences and on Luke's concern to point out the fulfillment of Jesus' predictions.

It has long been acknowledged that the empty tomb is the focus of Mark's final chapter in spite of the fact that the young man directs the women's attention to the reality of the resurrection before he indicates the empty tomb. The revelation of the resurrection is proclaimed; the empty tomb is demonstrated. The empty tomb is proffered as proof that Jesus is risen. As Lane writes, "The focus upon human inadequacy, lack of understanding and weakness throws into bold relief the action of God and its meaning."[17] The proclamation of verses 6 and 7 provides the contrast. In the final verse an empty tomb and a mistaken group of women provide a desolate picture for the end of a mission. By portraying these women in error in 16:1–5 and 8, the Markan author has concluded his narrative on a decisively negative note.

It hardly seems possible to assume with R.H. Lightfoot that the emotional responses of the women are a "gathering up" of emotions caused throughout the narrative by Jesus' messianic actions.[18] Emotional responses have been somewhat stereotyped throughout the gospel and the first reactions of these women fit that pattern. When they saw the stone rolled back and the young man in the white robe, "they were amazed." The verb is exethambēthēsan, a form of thambeō intensified by the prefix ek.[19] This intensive form is also used of Jesus in Gethsemane where he is described as distressed to the point of horror (14:33). The young man's admonition in verse 6, "Do not be amazed" (mē ekthambeisthe) seems to strengthen the meaning of extreme distress on the part of the women. Clearly, they are not made happy by this sequence of events.

In the final verse, the emotional reaction of the women is described as one of trembling and astonishment (tromos kai ekstasis). Reginald Fuller has pointed out, "Trembling and ecstasy are the usual biblical reaction to an angelophany."[20] This is the only use Mark makes of the word tromos. It is surely intended to describe extreme distress even to the point of causing physical manifestation. Moulton defines it as "fear, terror, agitation of mind."[21] Astonishment (ekstasis) is their other immediate reaction. The word, in the same form, is used to describe the response to the raising of Jairus' daughter (5:42). In a slightly different form it is used by Jesus' family to describe his condition (exēstē) (3:21). Its positive tone is not totally devoid of negative connotations.

A secrecy command from Jesus follows the raising of Jairus' daughter (5:42–43); a secrecy response by the women follows the proclamation of Jesus' resurrection by the young man at the tomb (16:8). In both, the human response to a commanded action is to be astonished. The structure of the sentence in verse 8, two parallel clauses each ending with an *enthymeme,* suggests that the trembling and astonishment were as much a response to the command to spread the message to the disciples and Peter (the content of the second part of the verse) as it was to the reality of the empty tomb and the young man with the message, the cause of the flight. When the reactions are considered together—amazement, trembling, astonishment—the groundwork has been laid for the climactic (ephobounto gar) (16:8).

If 16:8 is accepted as the intended ending of Mark's gospel, the decision must be made whether or not to stand with those who consider the women's flight and the fear which causes it as a "shocking reversal of expectations."[22] It then becomes necessary to try to find a reason for such a reversal. However, one can consider the ending totally consistent with a pattern found throughout the gospel. Lane finds the final action "thoroughly consistent with the motifs of astonishment and fear developed throughout the gospel."[23] Boomershine's study provides a lucid example of acknowledgment of the strongly negative element in Mark's gospel without acknowledgment of negation as a level of meaning.

Boomershine indicates that in the Markan writing *many* comments are used when offering an explanation of startling or puzzling actions.[24] Therefore, he judges that the readers of Mark are supposed to be startled and puzzled by the flight of the women. In another article, he maintains that the verb ephugen, used in 16:8 to describe the flight of the women, having also been used of the flight of the disciples in 14:50, and of the flight of the unidentified man in 14:52, "is set, therefore, in a strongly negative context."[25] After discussion of the women's silence as strongly inappropriate, he concludes that "the norms associated with the women's flight and silence are totally negative."[26] He then goes on to propose that the author had first created sympathy for these women and understanding of their response. He argues that the narrative comments in verse 8 are mitigating explanations of their failure. It is, in fact, tremendously difficult to find anything sympathetic or understanding in the final verse. Following the description of amazement to the point of terror in verses 5 and 6, the doubling of negatives (oudeni, ouden) in verse 8 seems to preclude any contrary judgment about the motive. The final and famous ephabounto gar is explanation, of course, but no more sympathetic and understanding than the description of the Gerasenes' fear at seeing the cured demoniac and asking Jesus to leave them (5:15-17) or of the disciples who respond to his coming to them walking on the sea and who fear (6:50) and fail to understand because their hearts are hardened (6:51-52).

There are so many obviously negative elements in the final chapter of Mark's gospel, and especially in the final verse, that attempts to explain them away seem highly inappropriate. There is a clear proclamation in verse 6 and a clear command in verse 7. Neither influences the women to anything except flight and the author patterns their flight upon that of the disciples and the young man: "The dominant tone of the ending is negative."[27] The ending makes a strong contribution to the contention that there is a total level of negation in Mark since it has no mitigating characteristics and is final. The women never understand, just as the disciples, family and officials of Judaism never understand. The author chose to end the narrative in total negation.

This, then, provides a climactic irony that depends in large part on its nature as dramatic irony. The reader knows that Jesus is Messiah and Son of God. He knows that Jesus has indeed risen and that the command to go into Galilee should be taken seriously. The reader knows that these events are fulfillments of the passion–resurrection prophecies. So the two levels of meaning end here, each with its own finality. On the human level, the level of seeing, hearing, perceiving and understanding, there is failure. Not even the heroic women who stood by the cross and assisted at the burial really believe in the resurrection. On the level of proclamation the outcome has been proclaimed: "he has risen . . . he is going before you to Galilee; there you shall see him, as he told you" (16:6–7). The reader knows that this proclamation portrays the true situation, since the document would not exist if that prediction had not been fulfilled:

> Simple ironies always function quite openly as correctives. One term of the ironic duality is seen, more or less immediately, as effectively contradicting, invalidating, exposing, or at the very least, modifying the other. In the light of greater awareness, or of prior or subsequent knowledge (sometimes supplied by the ironist himself), an assumed or asserted fact is shown not to be true, an idea or belief to be untenable, an expectation to be unwarranted, or a confidence to be misplaced.[28]

With some degree of narrative skill the Markan author has shown that the lack of Jesus' success with the people around him is contradicted by the knowledge that the reader possesses. This exemplifies the most basic element of every irony, the contrast between what is real and what is apparent. The women are added to the list of innocent victims of this irony, a list which includes Jesus' family and neighbors, his disciples and the officials of Judaism. The irony is sharp. Its victims are portrayed as unaware of their mistake, but the reader knows both elements of the dual presentation and is well aware of the effective contradiction of the level of the negation by the level of proclamation. The final chapter of Mark's gospel adds to the negative level both by what is included in it and by what is missing. It is only less definitive because it is limited to such a small part of the narrative.

The Treatment of Miracles

Accounts of miracles in Mark can illustrate both the affirmative and the negative levels of the narrative. Some of the miracles are totally and convincingly laudatory. Others demonstrate a tendency to mute details, thereby neutralizing some of the effect of the miraculous work. Sometimes this is so true that a narrative becomes hard to classify as a miracle either because the miraculous nature of the incident is not made clear or because of the very nature of the happening. Both the transfiguration narrative (9:2–8) and the walking on the sea incident (6:45–52) are unusual occurrences, but their literary characteristics suggest that they may be resurrection narratives retrojected into the life of Jesus. The transfiguration narrative will not be included here because it is treated elsewhere.[29] The walking on the sea will be treated because of its relationship to the feeding miracle and the similarities it bears to the other sea miracle in 4:35–41.

In this study of the treatment of miracles in Mark, seventeen pericopae will be considered. They are:

a. nine physical healings   1:29–31
                                   1:40–45
                                   2:1–12
                                   3:1–6
                                   5:21–24 and 35–43
                                   5:24–34
                                   7:31–37
                                   8:22–26
                                   10:46–52
b. four driving out of evil spirits 1:21–28
                                   5:1–20
                                   7:24–30
                                   9:14–29
c. two feedings   6:34–44
                                   8:1–10
d. two nature miracles   4:35–41
                                   6:45–52

This list excludes stories which have miraculous overtones but are not clearly presented as miracles—for example, the cursing of the fig tree, 11:12–14 and 20–26; the summaries, 1:32–34, 3:7–12, and 6:53–56. Also left untreated will be Jesus' ability to know incidents he does not witness, as in 6:48 and 9:33–35, and his ability to read people's motives, as in 2:5–8 and 9:10.

The seventeen pericopae dealing with events which can be considered miraculous function in a variety of relationships to the level of negation. Six of them, clearly affirmative, are presented without any effort to moderate their laudatory elements and, hence, can be seen to function totally on the affirmative level. This includes two incidents which result in an individual beginning his discipleship as did the leper who is cured in 1:40–45 and who "began to talk freely about it," and to spread the "news" and Bartimaeus in 10:46–52 who "followed him on the way." Both feeding stories, 6:34–44 and 8:1–10, are fully affirmative, although lacking any follow-up comments from the disciples or from the recipients. The healing of the deaf and dumb man in the Decapolis, 7:31–37, serves a distinctly affirmative purpose:

> Jesus can both open the ears and eyes of those who at present in the pagan world do not see or hear, and he can also do the same for those within the community who are deficient in sight or hearing in relation to what their faith means to them.[30]

In the first chapter, verses 21–28, Jesus drives out an unclean spirit. The fact that the spirit convulses the man and cries out with a loud voice is almost lost in the proclamation that he is the Holy One of God. The on-lookers are amazed mostly because he teaches with authority. So, this strongly proclamatory happening directs attention to a miraculous occurrence, to a proclamation of Jesus as "Holy One of God" and to recognition that he teaches with authority. Thus it is clear that these six pericopae function on the affirmative level and that they contribute significantly to the proclamation of Jesus as Son of God and as Messiah.

Another seven pericopae, almost as clearly affirmative and proclamatory as those already discussed, are muted to some degree by a variety of devices. The use of a negative exchange in the strongly affirmative calming of the sea (4:35–41) is one such device. The marvel of the calming of the sea is entwined with the rebuke of Jesus by the disciples, "Teacher, do you not care if we perish?" (4:38), and with Jesus' equally strong rebuke of his disciples, "Why are you afraid? Have you no faith?" (4:40). Attention is thus directed away from the awesome deed of driving out the evil spirit. However, attention returns to the affirmative level in the disciples' awe-struck question: "Who, then, is this, that even wind and sea obey him?" (4:41). So the pericope ends on a laudatory note.

The incident of Jesus' walking over the water in 6:45–51 may well be considered a retrojected post-resurrection narrative, or, perhaps,

the shaping of the miracle stories in the earthly life of
Jesus, especially under the influence of the divine man
concept, have provided traits which were later carried
over into the narration of the appearances.[31]

Either way, the story has a strong laudatory and affirmative
orientation. However, the final statement of the incident indicates a strongly negative element within the basically affirmative happening. The parallel text in Matthew concludes,
"Those in the boat worshiped him, saying, 'Truly you are the
Son of God' " (Matthew 14:33). Mark concludes, "For they did
not understand about the loaves, but their hearts were hardened" (6:52). It is the same hardness that had grieved Jesus
when the Pharisees objected to his healing on the sabbath (3:5).
A basically affirmative story is allowed to end on a decisively
negative note, in total opposition to Matthew's presentation
of the same incident (Matthew 14:24–33) which includes the
enigmatic but surely startling incident of Peter's walking on
the water.

The pericope of the expulsion of the demons from the
Gerasene demoniac also joins a negative occurrence to the
over-all effect of the strong Jesus overpowering evil spirits:

> the demoniac, healed of a legion of unclean spirits, is told
> to go and tell his people what the Lord has done for him.
> It is worth noting that Jesus tells him that his faith has
> healed him, and that the man wishes to follow him as a
> disciple: those who believe may proclaim what the Lord
> has done for them.[32]

The action of the townspeople in asking Jesus to depart from
them certainly negates some of the laudatory effect the incident might have had and mutes some of the over-all effect of
the story. Nonetheless, the narrative ends with the strong affirmation of the cured man who goes away to proclaim what
Jesus had done for him.

The cure of the woman with a hemorrhage (5:24–34) is

another highly affirmative incident. It has the characteristic features of a miracle story "description of the sufferer, the failure of the physicians, the cure and its public confirmation."[33] However, there are elements in this particular story which raise difficult questions. The motif of the touching of Jesus' garment, the fact that the woman felt in her body that she was cured, the rebuke of Jesus by his disciples, and the guilty reaction of the woman make the story somewhat obscure at the same time as they introduce negative elements. The detail of the touching of Jesus' garment by the woman may be intended to emphasize that Jesus has allowed himself to be touched by someone who is ritually impure. The question peremptorily asked by the disciples is decidedly negative, really a reprimand: "You see the crowd pressing around you, and yet you say, 'Who touched me?'" (5:31). They obviously have no understanding of what is transpiring. The fear and trembling experienced by the woman seem to be caused less by awe than by true fear that she will be punished for her action. However, the story ends on an affirmative note. The woman's faith has brought her healing. Peace, probably in the Semitic sense of well-being, is to be her lot. As Best has explained:

> Into the valediction of Jesus, "Go in peace," may be read a deeper meaning; peace is not merely health but peace with God, through the reconciliation that has taken place with him in healing and therefore in the restoration to the congregation of Israel.[34]

The cure of the daughter of the Syro-Phoenician woman (7:24–30) is mentioned as a fait accompli, not a wonderful work to be described in detail. The preceding verses, 7:1–23, have dealt with matters of ritual purity. In verse 24, Jesus enters Gentile territory and with what appears to be total disregard for laws of purity enters the house of a Gentile and performs a miracle at the request of a Gentile woman. This woman's behavior is in total contrast to the attitudes displayed by the Pharisees and scribes and even of his own disciples. She accepts the parable Jesus speaks about the bread of the children not being shared with the dogs. Hengel explains:

> She has taken it deep into herself, has understood it, and in understanding it has entered into the parable and answers in terms of it, developing the parable further: "But the dogs eat the scraps which the children drop under the table." And by doing this, by performing this act, by allowing herself to be taken up into the parable, by completely entering into the parable as Jesus has presented it to her—for this is not an act of understanding; it is nothing pedagogical—the demon has already departed from her daughter.[35]

The act of driving out the evil spirit receives somewhat less attention than the contrast between the arrogant rigidity of the Jewish officials, the lack of understanding on the part of the disciples and the humble sincerity of the Gentile woman. Her request is granted because of her humble faith.

In the Matthean parallel, the woman is described as having the same humble and sincere stance, even though Jesus has first refused to help with the harsh words, "I was sent only to the lost sheep of the house of Israel" (Matthew 15:24). Matthew heightens both of the focal points of this incident: the faith which merits a miracle as well as the humility of the woman. Mark's account is considerably muted by comparison.

Matthew 15:21–28	*Mark 7:24–30*
A Canaanite woman from that region	A woman—a Greek, a Syro-Phoenician birth
(she) cried, "O Lord, Son of David"	whose little daughter was possessed by an unclean spirit

Matthew 15:21–28	*Mark 7:24–30*
his disciples came up and began to entreat him, Get rid of her.	
	she begged him
"O woman, great is your faith! Be it done to you as you desire" and her daughter was healed instantly.	"for this saying you may go your way, the demon has left your daughter."

Clearly the Markan account is more subdued and muted but equally the incident praises the woman's sincerity and her humility. And it recounts a miraculous cure.

Somewhat similarly, the progressive opening of the eyes of the blind man of Bethsaida (8:22–26) is played against the lack of understanding by the disciples (8:14–21) much as the incident recorded in 7:31–37 played the progressive opening of the ears and loosening of the tongue of the deaf mute against the lack of understanding by the disciples in the controversy over law (7:1–23). The affirmation in the story, somewhat mitigated by the structural irony involved, is described by Lane:

> In this regard (healing as a promised action of God), Chapter 8:22–26 invites comparison with Chapter 7:31–37 where the theological point that the promised intervention of God has taken place in the ministry of Jesus is established by an allusion to Isa. 35:5f. and a confession of faith. (Chap. 7:32, 37)[36]

The impact of the opening of the blind man's eyes is muted by the contrast with the closed minds of the disciples and by the implied secrecy command at the end of the pericope: "Do not even enter the village" (8:26).

The final example of a strongly affirmative incident which includes some muting or distracting element can be found in 9:14–29, the cure of the demoniac boy. The incident is certainly a miracle story. However, its primary purpose is to demonstrate the comparative ease with which Jesus achieves that which the disciples could not do. The enigmatic aspect of verse 15 where the crowd is "amazed" at the fact of Jesus' coming is not found in the parallel texts. "Only in Mark, after the transfiguration, does the whole crowd become amazed."[37] This illustrates a Markan practice of attributing strong, but stereotyped emotional reactions.

The detailed description of the boy's condition (9:20–22) and of his cure (9:25–27), interrupted only in Mark (compare Matthew 17:14–18 and Luke 9:37–43) by a conversation about the necessity of belief, directs attention away from the affirmative, almost spectacular, account of this miracle. Jesus' entrance onto the scene occurs in the midst of an argument between the disciples and the scribes. Mark proceeds to describe the characteristics of the illness in much more graphic detail than either Matthew or Luke. Matthew labels the boy an epileptic and describes his falling into water and fire. Luke, more graphically, writes, "A spirit seizes him, and he suddenly cries out; it convulses him until he foams, and shatters him" (Luke 9:39). Mark provides a vividly graphic description: "whenever it seizes him, it dashes him down; and he foams and grinds his teeth and becomes rigid" (9:18) and "It has often cast him into the fire and into the water to destroy him" (9:22); and "after crying out and convulsing him terribly, it came out and the boy was like a corpse; so that most of them said, 'he is dead'" (9:26).

Jesus demands faith of the father of the boy. The passage is similar to the incident with the leper in 1:40–45 where the leper says, "If you will, you can make me clean." With no objection, Jesus says, "I will, be clean." In the incident with the demoniac boy's father, Jesus objects to the implication of "If you can do anything" (9:22), that is, that he might not be able to bring about the healing. In the earlier episode there is no such implication. It is apparent, then, that in two ways this author mutes the spectacular effect of the driving out of the evil spirit from the demoniac boy: the argument with the scribes, and the dialogue with the father about faith.

Two incidents, the cure of Peter's mother-in-law (1:29–31) and the cure of Jairus' daughter (5:21–24, 35–43), have ambiguous elements which mute their obviously laudatory intent. The cure of Peter's mother-in-law is so low-keyed that it really does not need to be taken as a miraculous action. The raising of Jairus' daughter is just ambiguous enough that it cannot clearly qualify as a resurrection story. The first incident has aready been treated.[38] The ambiguity in the story of Jairus' daughter lies in the word katheudei, which, it has been pointed out by several scholars, can be taken literally or figuratively, meaning the sleep of death or natural sleep.[39] Both Matthew (9:18–26) and Luke (8:49–56) make it clear that the girl had died and that the miracle was that of raising her from the dead. Mark's account lacks that clarity. As Taylor writes: "If, as is probable, Mark himself regarded the incident as one of resurrection, he has related the story with great objectivity in that another interpretation is possible."[40] The ambiguity results in a less forceful account than those in Matthew and Luke. Another occasion for a strongly laudatory and affirmative portrayal has been muted by the manner of presentation and in what seems to have been a deliberate manner.

Finally, two of the miracle accounts seem to become almost, but not quite, negated because of their predominantly polemical nature. The cures of the paralytic (2:1–12) and of the man with the withered hand (3:1–6) frame the series of incidents which portray growing opposition to Jesus. In the first incident (2:1–12), the scribes question in their hearts if Jesus has the right to forgive sins. In response, and to prove a point, he cures the paralytic. In the fifth and final incident of the series (3:1–6), the Pharisees are lying in wait to see if Jesus breaks the sabbath. Both incidents are so involved in the display of opposition that the miraculous nature of the events is somewhat muted.

In curing the paralytic (2:1–12), Jesus is almost taunting the scribes with his "crime." The cured man, however, disappears from the scene almost immediately without any mention of a reaction. His role has been fulfilled when he has been cured. The man with the withered hand (3:1–6) is lost in the description of the Pharisees' desire to accuse Jesus, in the rhetorical question which places them in a dilemma, and in Jesus' angry response to their hardness of heart. The result of the encounter—the Pharisees' and Herodians' intention to destroy him—would completely remove this incident from the level of affirmation except for the fact that it does, indeed, involve a miraculous cure.

With four different devices, the author of Mark has depicted miraculous incidents. As Achtemeier points out: "Mark continued the process of adapting and interpreting the miracle stories."[41] Six of these pericopae stand out as affirming the identity of Jesus as Messiah and Son of God, the one who works the wonders that Yahweh worked in the Hebrew scriptures: "We do not learn with certainty what Jesus thought of himself, although it is reasonable to think that he, as well as his followers, saw his miracle as testifying to his being a true messenger from or agent of God."[42] Other miraculous events add to this affirmation in spite of distractions and meanings which tend to minimize the laudatory effect. Two are muted to the point where the effect is ambiguous. Two are so polemical that they add something to the negative level. One of several factors which contribute to the negative level of Mark's gospel is, therefore, the manner in which the miracles are depicted.

The Limiting of Witness

The final example of devices used in the Markan narrative to mute the effect of an incident can be called the limiting of witnesses. This evidence is less definitive than the major arguments because in many instances a whole crowd is used to witness a miracle or to hear an instruction.[43] Therefore, it cannot be said that the Markan author always limits witnesses. He does so when he wishes to mute the effect of a particular incident. The evidence is quite straightforward.

At Jesus' baptism, where the voice from heaven proclaims him beloved Son, only Jesus saw (eiden) the heavens opened and the Spirit descending (1:10). It seems safe to assume that only he heard the voice (1:11) which proclaims him, since no other observer is present, with the possible exception of John. However, no indication is given that John is still present. No response of any kind is recorded.

The raising of Jairus' daughter, even with its ambiguous focus, at least comes close to being a resurrection narrative and, as such, is an important display of power. It is witnessed only by Peter, James, John and the parents of the child. The Lukan account, 8:51, includes the same observers as Mark's, but in Matthew's account the only mention of witnesses is in the words, "when the crowd had been put out" (Matthew 9:25). In Matthew there is no indication of anyone remaining in the room while Jesus raises the little girl. Matthew seems concerned to eliminate the mourners, since their purpose was to lament the death. He shows no other interest in enumerating witnesses. Mark also excludes the mourners but notes precisely that Peter, James, John and the parents are present. Luke has the same witnesses as Mark but makes the situation unclear by including conversation with the crowd after Jesus entered the house, having "permitted no one to enter with him except Peter, John, James and the child's parents" (8:51).

In the incident where Jesus walks on the sea and calms its power (6:45–52), only the small group of disciples who could fit into a boat witnessed the Yahweh-like manifestations of power. In the two incidents where Jesus performs a progressive opening of the ears, 7:31–37, or eyes, 8:22–26, he first takes the sufferer away from all observers; "and taking him aside from the multitude privately" (7:33), and "he took the blind man by the hand, and led him out of the village" (8:23). These incidents are found only in Mark and both reflect a fulfillment of the healings promised in Isaiah 35:4–5.

> Say to those whose hearts are frightened:
>   Be strong, fear not!
> Here is your God, he comes with vindication:
>   With divine recompense he comes to save you.
> Then will the eyes of the blind be opened,
>   the ears of the deaf be cleared.

Even though the Isaian passage is clearly proclamatory of the presence of God among his people, the Markan author limits the witnesses in both accounts.

In all three synoptic accounts, the witnesses to the transfiguration are carefully limited to Peter, James and John. Those who are privileged to hear the eschatological discourse in Mark are the same three, along with Andrew. They had been the first group of four called to follow. The hearers of similar eschatological discourses in Matthew 24:3–14 and Luke 21:5–19 are "the disciples." It is probable that Luke intended an extensive audience since the incident is preceded by the words, "In the hearing of all the people, he said to his disciples" (Luke 20:45). Again, only Mark seems determined to limit the number of hearers, thereby limiting the effect of the discourse.

Finally, in the empty tomb narrative (16:1–8), only three women are privileged to see the empty tomb and to hear the young man's message. They keep this knowledge to themselves.[44]

All of these incidents are related in some way to the affirmation of who Jesus is and all are muted by the narrative device of excluding large numbers of witnesses. It is a marked feature of this gospel that the author summons up a crowd almost at will and is careful to let the reader know just who is present at any particular time. He chose the witnesses to each action carefully. The device of limiting witnesses then, deliberately employed, limits or neutralizes some of the effects of the laudatory elements in this gospel.

Possible Evidence

There are three further points which add some strength to the contention that there is a negative level of meaning in the gospel of Mark. The role of the crowd, the passive portrayal of Jesus in key passages, and the commands to secrecy all add in some measure to this level. It has already been seen[45] that the Markan author uses audiences with skill and to serve the purposes he intends. He uses the crowd with great regularity.

The Role of the Crowd

In the narrative which precedes Chapter 11, crowds are involved nine times in incidents where Jesus is teaching (2:13; 3:32; 4:1; 4:36; 5:21; 6:34; 7:14; 8:34; 10:1). On one occasion a crowd is plainly seeking miracles (3:9-10). Twice a crowd is the occasion for compassion and a miraculous feeding by Jesus (6:34-44 and 8:1-10). A crowd is present at the cure of the paralytic (2:1-12), the cure of the woman with a hemorrhage (5:25-34), of the possessed boy (9:14-29) and of Bartimaeus (10:46-52). Clearly, the crowd is employed by Mark to witness those things which Jesus teaches and the miracles which he performs. Only in the two feeding stories does the crowd benefit directly from the miraculous action.

The author's use of the crowd changes in Chapter 11. There are three references in Chapters 11 and 12 ("for they feared him, because all the multitude [ho ochlos] was astonished at his teaching," 11:18, "they were afraid of the crowd [ton ochlon]," 11:32, "And they tried to arrest him, but feared the multitude [ton ochlon]," 12:12.) Here the crowd functions as a retarding factor, keeping the scribes and chief priests from taking action against Jesus. In a fourth reference in 12:37, the crowd is glad to hear Jesus destroy a scribal argument. The Markan author makes it clear that the officials have become fearful of the crowd.

In the early reference to a crowd in Chapter 14, a crowd comes to apprehend Jesus. This crowd is characterized as one "from the chief priests and the scribes and the elders" (14:43), and may be considered a specific group, not the multitude who normally followed Jesus. Nonetheless, the same word is now used for the first time to indicate those who oppose Jesus.

The crowd appears three times in Chapter 15. First, "the crowd came up and began to ask Pilate to do as he was wont to do for them" (15:8). They are seeking the release of a prisoner on the occasion of the feast. Historicity aside, the action quite possibly is not intended to indicate hostility toward Jesus, but a desire to obtain the release of Barabbas. Cranfield describes this crowd: "Probably supporters of Barabbas who had come to ask for his release."[46]

During the dialogue with Pilate (15:9–15), the crowd is manipulated by the chief priests. They turn against Jesus and call for his crucifixion. This reversal seems to have occurred with some ease. The crowd cries out against Jesus vehemently, even irrationally: "Crucify him, crucify him." They cannot produce a reason for such an execution, so they increase the vehemence of their demand. By this device the author places a large share of the blame for Pilate's final decision directly on the crowd which has been manipulated by the chief priests: "So, Pilate, wishing to satisfy the crowd ... " (15:15). The crowd has been used by the chief priests, and by the author, to become the focus of hostility toward Jesus.

The crowd, through this device, having been summoned up repeatedly to hear Jesus teach and to witness his miracles, in the end becomes the focal point of opposition to him. The

crowd is used at one point to retard the action of apprehend-
ing Jesus and at another to intimidate Pilate into delivering
Jesus up to be crucified. The word, then, seems intended to be
a tool for whatever purpose the author chooses to use it. To
whatever purpose, in the end the crowd is in opposition to
Jesus and part of the negative level of Chapter 15.

It has been suggested that Mark's use of the crowd is too
general to allow any conclusion about the force it might exert
in the final chapter.[47] Certainly the crowd is used in whatever
way the author chooses. One of those ways is to force a weak
and vacillating Pilate into the decision to crucify Jesus. There
was at work, of course, the motive of removing as much blame
as possible from the Romans. As E.P. Sanders has written:

> The Gospels are all influenced by the desire to incriminate
> the Jews and exculpate the Romans. The insistence of the
> crowd that Jesus be killed, despite Pilate's considering
> him innocent (Matt. 27:15–26; Mark 15:6–15; Luke
> 23:18–23; cf. John 18:38), shows this clearly enough.[48]

With a somewhat different orientation, D.E. Nineham had
earlier written on this tendency in Mark

> to emphasize the responsibility of the Jews (vv.11, 15a)
> whose hatred of Jesus was so completely unjustified that
> even a man like Pilate could see through it (vv. 10, 14), yet
> so strong and insenate that it overcame his persistent scru-
> ples (vv. 9, 12, 14, 15). Pilate acts against his better judg-
> ment; it is the Jews who must take the responsibility (cf.
> Matt. 27:24–25). This hatred was not confined to one class
> among the Jews (cf. the crowd, vv. 11 and 15), though the
> leaders, and particularly the priests (v. 11) were behind the
> popular rejection of Jesus.[49]

It is impossible to determine the identity of the crowd but it
is clear that the crowd is a negative force in the penultimate
chapter of Mark's gospel. The crowd which had been

attracted by Jesus' teaching and miracles is turned against him by those Mark believed represented official Judaism. There is no indication of any retreat from this rejection. It supplies an additional element to the level of negation.

The Passive Jesus

Another argument which brings some support to the thesis of a negative portrayal of Jesus is the passive picture of him which occurs in at least three key incidents, 1:1–13; 9:2–8; and 15:1–39. Chapter 1:1–13 has been discussed above.[50] It needs only to be observed that verse 1 contains a proclamation of the good news of Jesus Christ and verses 2 through 8 concern the prophecy-fulfillment and the forerunner, John. The first mention of Jesus occurs in verse 9 where he comes "from Nazareth of Galilee." From that point on, he is acted upon: he "was baptized" (9), he "saw the heavens opened" (10), he saw the Spirit descending and heard the voice which cried out (10–11). He was driven into the wilderness by the Spirit, was tempted, and was ministered to by angels (12–13). The only action Jesus performed in this entire introductory, proclamatory sequence was to come from Nazareth, the necessary prelude to the entire action. Otherwise, he is totally passive in this introduction.

The transfiguration account, 9:2–8, affords another example of passive portrayal of Jesus. Whether the pericope has historical elements or not, whether it is a totally symbolic story or not, whether it is a resurrection narrative retrojected into the life of Jesus or not,[51] it is certainly another proclamation of Jesus' identity and role. Lightfoot believes the incident was oriented toward the disciples:

> it takes place solely for the sake of the three disciples, "He was transfigured *before them*"; "there appeared *unto them* Elijah with Moses"; "there came a cloud over-

shadowing *them*": "this is my only Son, hear *ye* him";
"and suddenly looking around, they saw no one anymore,
save Jesus only *with themselves.*"⁵²

Even if one were to choose to debate that the incident is
"solely" for the benefit of the disciples, it is incontrovertible
that their role is important. As in the baptism, Jesus' only role
is to come to the scene, this second time bringing with him
three witnesses. Beginning with the word, "he was transfigured," Jesus assumes a completely passive role:

> He was transfigured (2)
> his garments became glistening (3)
> there appeared to them (4)
> a cloud overshadowed them (7)
> a voice came out of the cloud (7)

In verses 5 and 6, the active character is Peter. The action in
this narrative is caused by supernatural forces in verses 2, 3, 4,
and 7 and by Peter in verses 5 and 6. Jesus is acted upon in this
dramatic proclamation of his identity as Son of God. Lane
points out, "Jesus is himself the new Tabernacle of divine
glory."⁵³ A revelation of who Jesus is has been made to the
disciples, not by Jesus himself, but rather by supernatural
forces. Jesus is the agent through whom God is at work. While
this is surely an affirmation and a proclamation, it illustrates a
tendency to depict Jesus as object of the action rather than as
cause of it or even as participating actively in it. He resumes
activity on the way down from the mountain (9:9).

A final, enigmatic passage depicting Jesus as almost
totally passive occurs in the crucifixion narrative, 15:1–39. It
is, in fact, an account of events surrounding the crucifixion
rather than an account of the crucifixion itself. Of the thirty-
nine verses, only two, verses 24 and 25, actually describe the
crucifixion and another two, verses 34 and 37, describe Jesus'
death. In Matthew's account, ten verses are used to describe

the crucifixion (Matthew 27:35–44) and six to describe the death of Jesus (Matthew 27:45–50). All of the remaining verses in Matthew as well as in Mark describe incidents which surround the event. Mark describes Jesus before Pilate, the crowd's demand for Barabbas, the crowning with thorns, Simon of Cyrene, the inscription and the robbers, the mockery by the passers-by, the darkness and finally the rending of the temple veil and the centurion's confession. The events surrounding the execution are described in detail while the actual crucifixion and death are muted.

Jesus actually does only two things in Chapter 15 of Mark's account. He answers Pilate, "You have said so" (15:2), when asked if he is King of the Jews. And he cries out twice (15:34 and 15:37). Through all of the remainder of the chapter, Jesus is acted upon or actions take place around him. The author's attention is on matters other than Jesus' identity or glorification. In verses 1–15, he is obviously concerned about Pilate's reluctance to condemn Jesus and the role of the chief priests and scribes in forcing him to this. As Nineham notes:

> But even if the charge was political, various motives may have led to the making of it, e.g. Pharisaic horror at Jesus' laxity with regard to the Law, and scribal jealousy of an unauthorized teacher, though it is a curious fact that these motives, so very prominent earlier in the gospel, play virtually no part in Mark's account of the Passion.[54]

After Jesus had answered Pilate's first question, he lapsed into a silence which lasted until the moments immediately preceding his death. From 15:2 on, Jesus is the object of Pilate's indecision, of the chief priests' manipulation, and of the mockery of the Roman soldiers as well as of his countrymen who pass by the scene. He is equally the object of the derisively brought charge, "King of the Jews." This expression is used five times in Chapter 15; "the Christ, the King of Israel" is used once (15:32). The effect is described by Werner Kelber:

A survey of the title in its dramatic settings discloses a curiously ambiguous and ironic quality. Jesus' own response to Pilate's question (15:2) (sy legeis) remains obscure and is open to interpretations in an affirmative, negative, or ironic sense. Pilate's adoption of the title (15:9, 12) may be contemptuous, ironic or out of secret conviction. The salutation of the soldiers (15:18) creates a cruel mock scene. The titulus (15:26) is expressly designed to state the nature of the crime. The reaction of the guardians of the Jewish religion, finally, reflects open ridicule and establishment ideology (15:32). Is the title then affirmed or negated by Jesus' cross? For Mk, is Jesus the King or is he not the King?[55]

The irony involved in the charge that Jesus was "King of the Jews" has been described by several scholars.[56] Unquestionably, the readers have been informed that Jesus is King of the Jews but the Roman soldiers, the author of the inscription, the passers-by and the chief priests believe they are being derisively ironic by taunting a dying criminal with the title of King. The effect is a double irony. "But what of Mark as he overtly reports the irony ironically in his account of the crucifixion?"[57] But even the direction of this irony points away from Jesus to the mockers who taunt him and to the readers who see the double irony. Jesus remains the silent object of all this.

In the two previous examples of passivity in the portrayal of Jesus, the purpose was clearly to emphasize the divine proclamation of Jesus' identity. The passive portrayal of Chapter 15 is different. Its purpose is to assign blame for the crucifixion onto the chief priests and the fickle mob which is manipulated by them and to show Jesus as the object of men's evil activities. This portrayal of Jesus as passive places him at some distance from the conflict and makes him appear merely the victim of such circumstances as Pilate's releasing the wrong criminal, manipulation by the Jewish officials and the brutality of the Roman soldiers.

The Secrecy Commands

The secrecy commands are another device employed by the Markan author in order to produce a negative level of meaning. Those passages usually considered secrecy commands are:

1:25 But Jesus rebuked him, saying, "Be silent, and come out of him!"

1:44 "See that you say nothing to anyone; but go, show yourself to the priest . . ."

7:36 And he charged them to tell no one; but the more he charged them, the more zealously they proclaimed it.

1:34 And he would not permit the demons to speak, because they knew him.

3:12 And he strictly ordered them not to make him known.

5:43 And he strictly charged them that no one should know this, and told them to give her something to eat.

8:30 And he charged them to tell no one about him.

9:9 And as they were coming down the mountain, he charged them to tell no one what they had seen . . .

The first of these commands, when examined carefully, seems not to be involved with real secrecy at all. In the first chapter Jesus is pictured as expelling an unclean spirit from an unidentified man in the synagogue. The unclean spirit proclaims Jesus "the Holy One of God" (1:24). But Jesus will not allow this proclamation and he says, "Be silent and come out of him" (1:25). The command is part of the normal procedure for an exorcism,[58] and it is made quite clear that the other synagogue-goers had heard the proclamation and the exchange between Jesus and the spirit before the spirit is commanded to be silent. The incident is oriented toward the proclamation and the exclamation of the crowd about Jesus' teaching and his authority. It is not oriented toward concealment.

The second occurrence in the first chapter which cannot truly be considered a secrecy command is found at 1:44, "See that you say nothing to any one, but go, show yourself to the priest . . . " This command of Jesus reflects his consciousness of the requirement that the leper present himself before the high priest to have his cure certified. So, in order to fulfill the requirements of the law, the man is told to go *first* to the high priest before spreading word of the healing.[59] In neither of these cases is the purpose of the command to hide Jesus' identity or power. So neither should be called a secrecy command.

Strictly speaking, there are only six commands which can be called secrecy commands. In the seventh chapter the cure of the deaf mute is recorded. Jesus charges them to tell no one. The results are similar to those of the cure of the leper in 1:40–45. The cured leper went out to "spread the news" and the cured deaf mute and his companions respond to Jesus' charge to tell no one with "the more he charged them, the more zealously they proclaimed it" (7:36). In both instances the charge is ignored and the proclamation of who Jesus is thus is extended. "In both cases the event of the miracle is handed on by KERUSSEIN (proclaiming) so in both cases the breaking of the silence command is interpreted positively."[60]

Two secrecy commands, "and he would not permit the demons to speak, because they knew him" (1:34), and "he strictly ordered them not to make him known" (3:12), are directed to unclean spirits. The Markan author seems to intend that Jesus should not be publicly proclaimed Son of God by unclean spirits. Here, the secrecy commands are used to offset proclamations made by those who were either not supposed to make them or who were used by the author to proclaim Jesus in order to provide an opportunity for Jesus to silence the affirmation. It might be as simple as the fact that unclean spirits are not really appropriate carriers of such a proclamation. Whatever the reason, it seems clear in these two instances that the commands to secrecy are based upon the source of the proclamation. Unclean spirits know who Jesus is but they are not allowed to speak this. The two incidents seem to say much more about unclean spirits and their relationship with Jesus than with a desire to keep his identity hidden. Nonetheless, these are real secrecy commands.

There are three other secrecy commands in Mark's gospel. All occur immediately following a manifestation of great, even divine, power by Jesus:

a. Following the raising of the daughter of Jairus, "he strictly charged them that no one should know this" (5:43).

b. After the confession of Peter at Caesarea Philippi, "he charges them to tell no one about him" (8:30).

c. And descending from the mount of the transfiguration Jesus, "charged them to tell no one what they had seen until the Son of Man should have risen from the dead" (9:9).

The injunction to silence after the cure of Jairus' daughter raises several questions. A crowd had gathered to mourn the child's death. Jesus put them out after they had laughed at him. It seems quite impossible that "those who were with him" (Peter, James and John and the parents of the child) would have been able to keep the crowd from knowing about such a remarkable feat as the restoration of the child. The command that "no one know this" can hardly be taken seriously in such a context. There seems to be just a remote chance that these commands, especially in this pericope, have a meaning we have not discerned.

In the climactic episodes of the confession at Caesarea Philippi and the transfiguration, there seems to be a real effort to portray the results of the action as minimal or even nonexistent. After Peter has correctly proclaimed Jesus "the Christ," they (the disciples) are charged to tell no one about him. The injunction is followed immediately by a passion teaching which completes the shift of attention from the proclamation to something else. So the secrecy command functions as a precipitous closure on the proclamation before the passion teaching begins. The secrecy commands, then, fit the larger pattern of muted effects. Wrede's opinion that Mark's primary concern was to keep the messiahship of Jesus secret is not adequate to explain all of the evidence. The commands to secrecy can be seen making a contribution to the negative level of meaning in Mark's gospel.

There is no command involved but it is significant that neither of the nature miracles (4:35–41 and 6:45–52) evokes any significant recorded response. The two feeding stories (6:35–44 and 8:1–10) likewise evoke no recorded reaction. After each nature miracle, the boat crosses to the shore "on the other side." Compared to the result of the healing of one man with a withered hand, "The Pharisees went out, and immediately held counsel with the Herodians against him, how to destroy him," the response to the nature wonders is very much muted and almost completely neutralized. In addition to the use of secrecy commands, the use of minimized responses helps to mute many otherwise strong passages in Mark.

More support is added to the thesis of a negative level of meaning in Mark's gospel by the results of the use of these three devices. The crowd is used to dramatize the reversal of Jesus' influence with the Jewish people. The passive portrayals in key incidents are used to show Jesus as agent of God and to dramatize the forces of evil massed against him. The secrecy commands and structural devices used to mute specific wonders are part of a larger pattern of neutralizing the effects of Jesus' wonderful works.

NOTES

[1] See Mark 9:2–8; 8:31; 9:31 and 10:34.

[2] See Nestle-Aland, *Novum Testamentum*, pp. 147–149. W.R. Farmer, *The Last Twelve Verses of Mark*, NTSMS 25 (Cambridge: University Press, 1974). Norman R. Petersen, "When Is an End Not an End?" et al.

[3] Nestle-Aland, *Novum Testamentum*, pp. 147–149. B.F. Westcott and F.J.A. Hort, *The New Testament in the Original Greek* (Cambridge and London: Macmillan, 1881). Zerwick, *A Grammatical Analysis of the Greek New Testament*, pp. 165–167, et al.

[4] See summary in Metzger, *A Textual Commentary on the Greek New Testament*, pp. 121–128.

[5] Farmer, *The Last Twelve Verses of Mark*, pp. 121–128.

[6] John Dominic Crossan, "Empty Tomb and Absent Lord," in Kelber, *The Passion in Mark*, pp. 135–152. Thomas E. Boomershine and G.L. Bartholomew, "The Narrative Technique of Mark 16:8," *Journal of Biblical Literature* 100/2 (1981): 213–223.

[7] Lightfoot, *The Gospel Message of Mark*, p. 80.

[8] Bultmann, *The History of the Synoptic Tradition*, p. 285.

[9] Nineham, *Saint Mark*, p. 439.

[10] Kelber, *The Passion in Mark*, p. 150.

[11] Lane, *Commentary on the Gospel of Mark*, p. 589.

[12] Bultmann, *The History of the Synoptic Tradition*, p. 286.

[13] Theodore J. Weeden, *Traditions in Conflict* (Philadelphia: Fortress, 1971).

[14] Thomas E. Boomershine, "Mark 16:8 and the Apostolic Commission," *Novum Testamentum* 15 (1973): 81–113.

[15] John Dominic Crossan, "Empty Tomb and Present Lord," in *The Passion in Mark*, p. 152.

[16] Bultmann, *The History of the Synoptic Tradition,* p. 286.

[17] Lane, *Commentary on the Gospel of Mark,* p. 592.

[18] Lightfoot, *The Gospel Message of Mark,* p. 92.

[19] Moule, *An Idiom Book of New Testament Greek,* p. 88.

[20] Reginald H. Fuller, *The Formation of the Resurrection Narratives* (New York: Macmillan, 1971), p. 53.

[21] Harold K. Moulton, *The Analytical Greek Lexicon Revised* (Grand Rapids: Zondervan, 1977).

[22] For an excellent summary of both sides of this question see Boomershine, "Mark 16:8 and the Apostolic Commission."

[23] Lane, *Commentary on the Gospel of Mark,* p. 591.

[24] Boomershine and Bartholomew, "Narrative Technique of Mark 16:8," p. 213.

[25] Boomershine, "Mark 16:8 and the Apostolic Commission," p. 229.

[26] Ibid.

[27] Ibid. p. 230.

[28] Muecke, *the Compass of Irony,* p. 23.

[29] See below in this chapter.

[30] Best, *Mark: The Gospel as Story,* p. 62.

[31] Fuller, *The Formation of the Resurrection Narratives,* p. 163.

[32] Hooker, *The Message of Mark,* p. 61.

[33] Taylor, *The Gospel according to St. Mark,* p. 289.

[34] Best, *The Temptation and the Passion: The Markan Soteriology,* p. 107.

[35] Hengel, *Studies in the Gospel of Mark,* pp. 97–98.

[36] Lane, *Commentary on the Gospel of Mark,* p. 286.

[37] John R. Donahue, *Are You the Christ? The Trial Narrative in the Gospel of Mark* (Missoula: SBL Dissertation Series 10, 1972), p. 66.

[38] See above, Chapter 3.

[39] Taylor, *The Gospel according to St. Mark,* p. 295. Lohmeyer, *Das Evangelium des Markus,* p. 106 et al.

[40] Taylor, *The Gospel according to St. Mark,* p. 295.

[41] Achtemeier, *Mark,* p. 78.

[42] Sanders, *Jesus and Judaism,* p. 173.

[43] For the uses of the word "ochlos" see Kittel, *Theological Wordbook of the New Testament,* Vol. III, I–1, pp. 586–587.

[44] See above in this chapter.

[45] See above in this chapter.

[46] Cranfield, *The Gospel according to Mark,* p. 450.

[47] Taylor, *The Gospel according to St. Mark,* p. 581.

[48] Sanders, *Jesus and Judaism,* p. 298.

[49] Nineham, *Saint Mark,* p. 412.

[50] See above Chapter 4.

[51] Lightfoot, *The Gospel Message of Mark,* pp. 43f. Bultmann, *The History of the Synoptic Tradition,* pp. 259–260. Rudolf Pesch, *Das Evangelium der Urgemeinde,* Auflage Februar, 1982 (Basel: Herder Freilburg, 1982), p. 112.

[52] Lightfoot, *The Gospel Message of Mark,* p. 44.

[53] Lane, *Commentary on the Gospel of Mark,* p. 321.

[54] Nineham, *Saint Mark,* p. 411.

[55] Kelber, "The Hour of the Son of Man and the Temptation of the Disciples," pp. 45–46.

[56] Booth, *The Rhetoric of Irony,* pp. 28–29.

[57] Ibid. p. 28.

[58] Nineham, *Saint Mark,* pp. 75–76. Lane, *Commentary on the Gospel of Mark,* p. 75. Achtemeier, *Mark* p. 80.

[59] See Leviticus 13 and 14 and *The Mishnah,* Negaim, 3:1, p. 678.

[60] Ulrich Luz, "The Secrecy Motif and the Markan Christology," in Christopher Tuckett, ed., *The Messianic Secret* (London: SPCK, 1983), p. 79.

Chapter 7

CONCLUSIONS

. . . ———————————————————————————— . . .

It is now possible to reach some conclusion about the thesis of a level of negation in Mark's gospel and to discuss some corollaries to this thesis. It has been shown that a unifying artistic principle, the creation of two levels of meaning, is at work in the Markan gospel to the point that it is accurate to call this gospel a narrative. Norman Petersen concluded cogently:

> Granted that Mark used a vast amount of pre-shaped material, including narratives with their own range of points of view, the rhetorical consistency of his own narrative is nothing short of remarkable. True, the rhetorical system is of the simplest sort—that of the third person, omniscient and intrusive point of view and voice. Yet, Mark has produced an integral system and, for this reason, it is necessary to read his Gospel as a narrative, not as a redaction.[1]

The distinction between narrative and redaction is essential to the thesis of this study.

To read Mark as a redaction is to read the incidents as separate, pre-existing entities seamed together by an editor. To read Mark as a narrative is to recognize that a consistent technique is used throughout on each of the levels and that one narrative world has been thus created. So many narrative structures have been proposed as basic to the meaning structure of Mark[2] that the conclusion of Dibelius that the composers of the gospels are "primarily collectors, vehicles of tradition, editors"[3] must be rejected. Some weight may be added to the proof that Mark is a narrative by consideration of the level of negation which pervades the gospel. This level of meaning, separate from but interrelated with the proclamatory level, is a narrative device and, since it is found throughout the entire narrative, strengthens the narrative structure. This negative level should not be subsumed into the affirmative level. The Markan author has created a narrative world in which a highly unsuccessful Jesus is portrayed concomitantly with a supernaturally proclaimed Messiah and Son of God.

The validity of the method employed in this study rests upon the validity of the distinction made between redaction and narrative. When Mark's gospel is accepted as a narrative, the form critical and redaction critical methods can be suspended and the gospel can be studied as a literary construct. To study Mark as a narrative is to assume that a true author, using materials which have been considered traditional, fashioned some originally distinct stories into a form for which he determined unifying themes and which he fashioned into an artistic whole.

The presence of negative, muting, neutralizing factors in the Markan gospel adds another element to the consideration of devices used by the Markan author to create a narrative world. The narrative line, that is, the development of the story from Jesus' first appearance, through the miracles, teachings, misunderstandings to the angelophany at the empty tomb, step-by-step creates the narrative world. The story moves inexorably toward crucifixion at the same time that it repeatedly reveals Jesus as Messiah and Son of God. While one level is moving toward total rejection, the other level is using proclamation, making statements without proof and offering no motivation for those actions which imply belief. This gospel is a literary construct which the author fashioned in the light of his own literary and theological presuppositions, one of which is the level of negation.

The demonstration that there are two levels of meaning in Mark is the content of Chapter 3 of this study. The affirmative level begins with the first words of the gospel, "The beginning of the gospel of Jesus Christ, Son of God" (1:1), and proceeds through a series of similar proclamations and supporting actions, and miraculous healings, and feedings and calmings of the sea, and teaching with authority. These laudatory aspects of the portrait tend to proclaim rather than to explain and, in many instances, evoke no recorded response. This is an important part of the Markan portrait of Jesus. It pervades from the initial verse, through the climactic confession at Caesarea Philippi and transfiguration, and closes with two important proclamations, "Truly this man was the Son of God" (15:39) and "He has risen" (16:6).

The negative level is equally complete and compelling. It begins with the comparison to John the Baptizer and the passive portrayal of Jesus in the introductory incidents (1:2–13), is reinforced by the passivity of Jesus in the transfiguration (9:2–8), and the trial narrative (15:1–39), and is substantiated by the failure of all those around Jesus to understand what he says and what he does and by the total abandonment that he ultimately experiences. This level comes to a fittingly negative closure when the women, having run off, "said nothing to anyone, for they were afraid" (16:8). The story ends on a decisively negative note which completes the level of lack of understanding and failure to perceive.

To understand this negative level it is necessary to examine the relationship of Jesus to John the Baptizer which is assumed more than proven, the extension throughout the narrative of the theme of rejection by those Mark understood to represent official Judaism, by the continuing and unrescinded incomprehension of the chosen disciples, by the definitive rejection of his family, and by the final failure of the women who had followed him with courage and devotion. This negative direction is deepened by the final rejection by the crowd, by Jesus' passivity, by the commands to secrecy, by the limiting of witnesses to significant actions and by the devices used in the descriptions of miraculous incidents. So, the carefully developed narrative line extends through the entire story and is regularly deepened by muting and neutralizing devices.

The use of two levels of meaning results in dramatic irony. The reader and the narrator know from the very first verse who Jesus is. The characters in the story do not know who he is. The dramatic irony pervades the entire narrative and is the factor which holds the two levels together. The intense negation, especially that of the final two chapters, would destroy the affirmative level had the narrator not already made it clear who this protagonist really is. It is the knowledge that the narrator shares with the reader that holds the two levels in tension. The dramatic irony, therefore, is the literary device which enables the author to bring much strongly negative material into the composition without causing it to destroy the hero.

The use of negative devices is so pervasive and so compelling that it constitutes an antithesis to the basic proclamation made in the gospel. The existence of the negative level invalidates Philip Schuler's contention that "One can hardly deny to Mark, Luke and John, for example, Matthew's focus on the bios of Jesus."[4] The scarcity of topoi alone makes this position untenable. The proclamations of who Jesus is are muted by scarcity of witnesses, or by secrecy commands, or by lack of comprehension. Jesus summons disciples who follow without question but who never understand. He attracts crowds who assemble with great regularity but with no recorded motivation except a desire for miracles. He performs miracles, some of which remain without recorded response, some of which are muted to a significant extent, some of which are almost totally devoid of affirmation. Jesus teaches with authority but no one understands. He is portrayed as a true leader, disciples follow him when he calls, crowds follow and press upon him and make demands on him. The same crowd is manipulated to cry for his crucifixion. All of his followers run away. On two occasions Jesus feeds large numbers of people, and on neither occasion is there any type of response recorded. On two other occasions, he controls the sea. On one of those occasions, after Jesus has upbraided his disciples for their lack of faith, their response is simply to question who he is. On the other occasion, it is to fail to understand. Jesus predicts his own future suffering, death and resurrection on three occasions. On the first occasion Peter begins to rebuke him; on the second, the response is lack of understanding and fear; on the third, James and John approach and ask to share his glory. On all three occasions real comprehension is lacking. The eschatological discourse, shared with the chosen four disciples, ends with a series of warnings but there is no indication of a response or of understanding. In the final incident of Mark's narrative, three women who have not understood at all approach the tomb and are told the good news that Jesus has risen and will be seen by his disciples in Galilee. They do nothing about it. Affirmative passages seem to be negated or muted.

It is simply impossible to ignore the effects of such a pervasive and intensive use of negating, muting and neutralizing elements on the meaning structure of this narrative. It seems to say that, indeed, there is here proclamation and action which substantiate Jesus' identity, the meaning of his life, death and resurrection. The negative elements, so emphatically presented, destroy any easy acceptance of the affirmative level. The proclamations must be seen, heard, perceived, understood, believed, precisely as proclamations. They are not proven by indisputably miraculous signs. They are not supported by a description of a loyal band of followers nor by a change in the operation of the religious establishment. Even when a spectacular event occurs, it never produces any affirmative response at all. The reader of Mark's gospel is going to have to base his belief, if such he has, on unproven proclamations that Jesus is Messiah and Son of God. In other words, faith in Jesus is just that—faith.

NOTES

[1] Norman R. Peterson, "Point of View in Mark's Narrative," *Semeia* 12 (1978): 118.

[2] See examples above in Chapter 1.

[3] Dibelius, *From Tradition to Gospel,* p. 3.

[4] Shuler, *A Genre for the Gospels,* p. 109.

Bibliography

WORKS CITED OR QUOTED

Achtemeier, Paul J. *Mark.* Proclamation Commentaries. Philadelphia: Fortress, 1975.

Aristotle. *On Poetry,* trans. S.H. Butcher, Library of Liberal Arts, Vol. 6. Indianapolis: Bobbs-Merrill, 1956.

———. *The Art of Rhetoric,* Eng. trans. by J.H. Freese. Loeb Classical Library, Vol. 22. Cambridge: Harvard University Press, 1947.

Auerbach, Erich. *Mimesis.* New York: Doubleday, 1953.

Barr, David L. *Toward a Definition of Genre.* Florida State University Ph.D. dissertation, 1974.

Beardslee, William A. *Literary Criticism of the New Testament.* Philadelphia: Fortress, 1970.

Best, Ernest. *Mark: The Gospel as Story.* Edinburgh: T. and T. Clark, 1983.

———. *The Temptation and the Passion: The Markan Soteriology.* Cambridge: Cambridge University Press, 1965.

Blass, F. and A. Debrunner. *A Greek Grammar of the New Testament and Other Early Christian Literature,* a translation and revision of the ninth-tenth German edition incorporating supplementary notes of S. Debrunner by Robert W. Funk. Chicago: University of Chicago Press, 1961.

Blevins, James L. *The Messianic Secret in Markan Research 1901–1976.* Washington: University Press of America, 1981.

Boomershine, Thomas E. "Mark 16:8 and the Apostolic Commission," *Journal of Biblical Literature* 100/2 (1981) 225–239.

Boomershine, Thomas E. and G.L. Bartholomew, "The Narrative Technique of Mark 16:8" *Journal of Biblical Literature* 100/2 (1981): 213–223.

Booth, Wayne E. *A Rhetoric of Irony*. Chicago: University of Chicago Press, 1974.

Bratcher, Robert G. and Eugene A. Neda. *A Translator's Handbook on the Gospel of Mark*. London: United Bible Societies, 1981.

Brown, Harry and John Milstead. *Patterns in Poetry*. Glenview: Scott, Foresman and Co., 1968.

Brown, Raymond E. *The Birth of the Messiah*. New York: Doubleday, 1977.

Bultmann, Rudolf. *The History of the Synoptic Tradition*, trans. John Marsh, revised ed. New York: Harper and Row, 1968.

Burkill, T.A. "Mysterious Revelation," in Christopher Tuckett, *The Messianic Secret*, pp. 44–48.

Cartlidge, David R. and David L. Dungan. *Documents for the Study of the Gospels*. Philadelphia: Fortress, 1980.

Charlesworth, James H. *The Old Testament Pseudepigrapha*. New York: Doubleday, 1983.

Cook, Michael J. *Mark's Treatment of the Jewish Leaders*. Leiden: Brill, 1978.

Cranfield, C.E.B. *The Gospel According to Mark*. Cambridge: University Press, 1959.

Crossan, John Dominic. "Empty Tomb and Absent Lord," in Werner Kelber, *The Passion in Mark*, pp. 135–152.

Dahl, Nils A. *The Crucified Messiah and Other Essays*, Minneapolis: Augsburg Press, 1974.

Daube, David. "The Earliest Structure of the Gospels," *New Testament Studies* 5 (1958–1959): 174–187.

Dewey, Joanna. *Markan Public Debate*. Chico: Scholars Press, 1980.

Dibelius, Martin. *From Tradition to Gospel*, trans. B.L. Woolf. London: Nicholson and Watson, 1934.

Dodd, C.H. *About the Gospels.* Cambridge: Cambridge University Press, 1950.

Donahue, John R. *Are You the Christ?* Missoula: SBL Dissertation Series 10, 1973.

―――. "The Neglected Factor in the Gospel of Mark," *Journal of Biblical Literature* 101 (December 1982): 563–594.

Doughty, Darrell J. "The Authority of the Son of Man (Mk. 2:1–3:6)," *Zeitschrift fur die Neutestamentliche Wissenschaft* 74 (1983): 161–181.

Farmer, William R. *The Last Twelve Verses of Mark.* NTSMS 25. Cambridge: Cambridge University Press, 1974.

―――. *The Synoptic Problem.* New York: Macmillan, 1964.

Fowler, Robert M. *Loaves and Fishes.* SBL Dissertation Series 54. Missoula: Scholars Press, 1981.

Frye, Northrop. *The Great Code: The Bible and Literature.* Toronto: Academic Press, 1981.

Fuller, Reginald H. *The Formation of the Resurrection Narratives.* New York: Macmillan, 1971.

―――. *The Mission and Achievement of Jesus.* London: SCM, 1967.

Gnilka, Joachim. *Das Evangelium nach Markus.* Zürich: Benzinger Verlag, Auflage, 1978.

Grassi, J.A. "The Eucharist in the Gospel of Mark," *American Ecclesiastical Review* 168 (1974): 595–608.

Greer, Rowan A. *Origen.* New York: Paulist Press, 1979.

Hahn, Ferdinand. *The Titles of Jesus in Christology.* New York: World, 1963.

Hawkin, David J. "The Incomprehension of the Disciples in the Markan Redaction," *Journal of Biblical Literature* 91 (1972): 491–500.

Hengel, Martin, *Studies in the Gospel of Mark.* Philadelphia: Fortress, 1985.

Hooker, Morna D. *The Message of Mark.* London: Epworth, 1983.

Horstmann, Maria. *Studien zur Markenischen Christologie.* Münster: Aschendorffschen Verlagsbuchhandlung, 1969.

Huck, Albert. *Synopsis of the First Three Gospels.* Ninth edition revised by Hans Lietzmann. Eng. ed. by F.L. Cross. Oxford: Blackwell, 1972.

Iser, Wolfgang. *The Implied Reader.* Baltimore: Johns Hopkins University Press, 1974.

Johnson, Sherman E. *The Gospel according to St. Mark.* London: Black, 1972.

Josephus, *Jewish Antiquities,* trans. L.H. Feldman. Loeb Classical Library, Vol. 10. Cambridge: Harvard University Press, 1965.

Juel, Donald. *Messiah and Temple: The Trial of Jesus in the Gospel of Mark.* SBL Dissertation Series 31. Missoula: Scholars Press, 1977.

Kelber, Werner H. "From Passion Narrative to Gospel," in Werner H. Kelber, ed., *The Passion in Mark,* pp. 153–180. Philadelphia: Fortress, 1976.

———. "The Hour of the Son of Man and the Temptation of the Disciples," in Werner H. Kelber, *The Passion in Mark.* Philadelphia: Fortress, 1976, pp. 41–60.

———. *Mark's Story of Jesus.* Philadelphia: Fortress, 1979.

———. *The Passion in Mark.* Philadelphia: Fortress, 1976.

Kennedy, George A. *New Testament Interpretation through Rhetorical Criticism.* Chapel Hill: University of North Carolina Press, 1984.

Kermode, Frank. *The Genesis of Secrecy: On the Interpretation of Narrative.* Cambridge: Harvard University Press, 1979.

Kingsbury, Jack Dean. *The Christology of Mark.* Philadelphia: Fortress, 1983.

Kittel, G. *Theological Wordbook of the New Testament,* Vol. III (Eng. trans. 1964). Grand Rapids: Eerdmans, 1964.

Klausner, Joseph. *Jesus of Nazareth,* trans. Herbert Danby. New York: Menorah, 1925.

Klosterman, Erich. *Das Markusevangelium,* fünfte Auflage. Tübingen: Mohr, 1971.

Lane, William. *Commentary on the Gospel of Mark.* Grand Rapids: Eerdmans, 1974.

Lightfoot, R.H. *The Gospel Message of Mark.* London: University Press, 1950.

Lohmeyer, Ernst. *Das Evangelium des Markus,* 17. Auflage Göttingen: Vandenhoeck and Ruprecht, 1957.

Loisy, Alfred E. *Les Évangiles Synoptiques,* 2 vols. Paris: Ceffonds, 1907.

Luz, Ulrich, "The Secrecy Motif and the Markan Christology," in Christopher Tuckett, ed., *The Messianic Secret,* pp. 75–96. London: SPCK, 1983.

Marxsen, Willi. *Mark the Evangelist,* trans. James et al. New York: Abingdon, 1969.

Meagher, John C. *Clumsy Construction in Mark's Gospel.* Toronto: Mellon, 1979.

Metzger, Bruce M. *A Textual Commentary on the Greek New Testament,* 3rd edition. United Bible Societies, 1971.

Meye, Robert P. *Jesus and the Twelve.* Grand Rapids: Eerdmans, 1968.

Meyer, Ben. F. *The Aims of Jesus.* London: SCM, 1979.

The Mishnah. trans. Herbert Danby. Oxford: Oxford University Press, 1933.

Moffatt, James, *An Introduction to the New Testament.* Edinburgh: T. and T. Clark, 1928.

Moule, C.F.D. *The Birth of the New Testament.* San Francisco: Harper and Row, 1982.

―――. *The Gospel according to Mark.* Cambridge: Cambridge University Press, 1965.

―――. *An Idiom Book of New Testament Greek.* Cambridge: Cambridge University Press, 1953.

Moulton, Harold K. *The Analytical Greek Lexicon Revised,* 1978 edition. Grand Rapids: Zondervan, 1977.

Muecke, Douglas C. *The Compass of Irony*. London: Methuen, 1969.

Muilenburg, James, "Form Criticism and Beyond," *Journal of Biblical Literature* 88 (1969): 1–18.

Neirynck, Frans. *Duality in Mark*. Leuven: University Press, 1972.

Nestle-Aland. *Novum Testamentum Graece*, 26. neu bearbeitete Auflage. Stuttgart: Deutsche Bibelstiftung, 1979.

Nineham, Dennis E. *Saint Mark*. Baltimore: Penguin, 1963.

Perrin, Norman, "The High Priest's Question and Jesus' Answer," in Werner H. Kelber, *The Passion in Mark*, pp. 80–95. Philadelphia: Fortress, 1976.

————. *What Is Redaction Criticism?* Philadelphia: Fortress, 1969.

Pesch, Rudolf. *Das Evengelium der Urgeneinde*. Auflage Februar 1982. Basel: Herder Freiburg, 1982.

Petersen, Norman R. "Point of View in Mark's Narrative," *Semeia* 12 (1978): 97–119.

————. "When Is the End Not the End? Literary Reflections on the Ending of Mark's Narrative," *Interpretation* 34 (April 1980): 151–166.

Philo. *On Moses*, trans. F.H. Colson. Loeb Classical Library, Vol. 6. Cambridge: Harvard University Press, 1966.

Plutarch. *The Parallel Lives*, Eng. trans. B. Perrin. Loeb Classical Library, Vols. 1–10. Cambridge: Harvard University Press, 1960.

Reiser, Marius. *Syntax und Stil des Markusevangeliums*. Tübingen: Mohr, 1984.

Rhoads, David. "Narrative Criticism and the Gospel of Mark," *Journal of the American Academy of Religion* 50 (September 1982): 411–432.

Rhoads, David and Donald Michie. *Mark as Story*. Philadelphia: Fortress, 1982.

Rigaux, Béda. *Témoignage de l'évangile de Marc*. Bruges: Desclée de Brouwer, 1965.

Robbins, Vernon K. *Jesus the Teacher*. Philadelphia: Fortress, 1984.

Robinson, James M. *The Problem of History in Mark*. London: SCM, 1957.

Sanders, E.P. *Jesus and Judaism*. London: SCM, 1985.

Schatkin, Margaret A. and Paul W. Harkins. *The Fathers of the Church*. Washington: Catholic University of American Press, 1985.

Schmid, Josef. *The Regensburg New Testament: The Gospel according to Mark*. New York: Alba House, 1968.

Schmidt, Karl Ludwig. *Der Rahmen de Geschichte Jesu*. Darmstadt: Wissenschaftliche Buckgesellschaft, 1969.

Schweizer, E. *The Good News according to Mark,* trans. D. Madvig. Richmond: John K. Knox Press, 1970.

Shipley, Joseph T. *Dictionary of World Literature*. Totowa, New Jersey: Littlefield, Adams and Co., 1953.

Shuler, Philip L. *A Genre for the Gospels*. Philadelphia: Fortress, 1982.

Smith, Morton. *Jesus the Magician*. New York: Harper and Row, 1978.

Styler, G.M., "The Priority of Mark," in C.F.D. Moule, *The Birth of the New Testament,* pp. 285–316. San Francisco: Harper and Row, 1982.

Talbert, Charles H. *What Is a Gospel?* London: SPCK, 1978.

Tannehill, Robert C. "The Disciples in Mark: The Function of a Narrative Role." *Journal of Religion.* 57 (1977): 386–405.

———. "The Gospel of Mark as Narrative Christology," *Semeia* 16 (1979): 57–96.

Taylor, Charles. *The Sayings of the Jewish Fathers*. New York: KTAV, 1969.

Taylor, Vincent. *The Gospel according to St. Mark,* 2nd edition. New York: Macmillan, 1966.

Tresmontant, Claude. *A Study of Hebrew Thought*. New York: Desclée, 1959.

Trocmé, Etienne. *The Formation of the Gospel According to Mark.* London: SPCK, 1963.

Tuckett, Christopher. *The Messianic Secret.* Philadelphia: Fortress, 1983.

Tyson, J.B. "The Blindness of the Disciples in Mark," *Journal of Biblical Literature* 80 (1961): 261–268.

Via, Dan O., Jr., *Kerygma and Comedy in the New Testament.* Philadelphia: Fortress, 1975.

Vorster, W.S., "Kerygma/History and the Gospel Genre," *New Testament Studies* 29 (1983): 87–92.

Votaw, Clyde Weber. *The Gospels and Contemporary Biographies in the Greco-Roman World,* 1915 reprint. Philadelphia: Fortress, 1970.

Weeden, Theodore J. *Traditions in Conflict.* Philadelphia: Fortress, 1971.

Wellhausen, Julius. *Einleitung in die drei ersten Evangelien.* Berlin: Georg Reimer, 1905.

Westcott, Brooke F. and Fenton J.A. Hort. *The New Testament in the Original Greek.* Cambridge and London: Macmillan, 1881–1882.

Westerholm, Stephen. *Jesus and Scribal Authority.* Lund: Gleerup, 1978.

Wrede, William. *Das Messiasgeheimnis in den Evangelien.* Göttingen: Vandenboeck and Ruprecht, 1901.

Zerwick, Max and Mary Grosvenor. *A Grammatical Analysis of the Greek New Testament,* unabridged, revised edition in one volume. Rome: Biblical Institute Press, 1981.

Subject Index

Proem, 61
prophet, 24, 65, 70–71, 98,
   118, 128, 129, 132

quest for the historical Jesus,
   vii

redaction criticism, viii, ix,
   2, 4–7, 15, 170, 171
resurrection narratives, lack
   of, 30, 48, 136–137, 138
resurrection narratives,
   retrojected, 144, 146, 152,
   159
rhetoric, 14, 62, 72, 74, 89
rhetorical devices, 3, 5, 6, 25,
   30, 61, 62, 65, 67, 69, 76,
   82
rhetorical questions, 37, 43,
   75–79, 92, 115, 125
ritual purity, 84, 85, 108–109
Roman centurion, 29, 77,
   172

sabbath, 35, 38, 50, 77–78,
   83, 97, 127, 129, 147, 152
Sadducees, 42, 44, 73, 74, 92,
   93, 94, 95, 114
Sanhedrin trial, 46, 76, 96–
   97, 98, 99
scribes, 35, 41, 44, 52, 73–77,
   79, 80–83, 85, 88, 92, 94–
   96, 98, 123–125, 131, 147,
   149, 151, 152, 153, 157,
   161

scribes and Pharisees, 23, 73,
   79, 83, 85–86, 88
secrecy commands, 1, 30,
   141, 150, 156, 163–166,
   172
secular mashal, 129
socio-rhetorical forms, 19, 27
Son of David, 55, 91, 94, 95
Son of God, 12, 19, 20, 24,
   25, 27–29, 33, 34, 39, 40,
   44, 56, 61, 66, 97, 107,
   121–122, 125, 132, 143,
   146, 147, 153, 160, 164,
   171, 172, 174
Son of Man, 19, 27, 76–77,
   165
Son of Mary, 128
sources, 7–8, 69, 82, 154, 159
Spirit, 33, 55, 64, 65, 67, 68,
   82, 129, 154, 159
story telling, 6
structural oppositions, 18
subsuming, 26, 27, 29, 171
summaries, 8, 37–39, 40, 72,
   84, 121, 145
symbolism, 12, 127
synoptic problem, viii, 7–9
Syro-Phoenician woman, 44,
   55, 77, 84, 110, 148

teaching, 34, 35, 37, 42–43,
   44, 75, 84, 108, 172, 173
temptations, 68–70
testimony texts, 62
text, qua text, 1–7
thematic oppositions, 46